Creative Worship 2

Other Wood Lake Books study and worship resources by Ian Price

A Sensual Faith: Experiencing God Through Our Senses

Spirit of Life: Five Studies to Bring Us Closer to the Heart of God

Creative Worship: Services from Advent to Pentecost

Services for Special Days

Creative Worship 2

Compiled & Edited by Ian Price

WOOD LAKE BOOKS

CREATIVE WORSHIP 2 was first published in Australia with the title *All God's People Worship*, by MediaCom Education Inc.

Wood Lake Books editor: Mike Schwartzentruber
Cover design: Margaret Kyle
Cover art: Barbara Houston, copyright © Wood Lake Books, 2002

Wood Lake Books acknowledges the financial support of the Government of Canada through the Book Publishing Industry Development Program (BPIDP) for our publishing activities.

At Wood Lake Books, we practice what we publish, being guided by a concern for fairness, justice, and equal opportunity in all our relationships with employees and customers. We recycle and reuse and encourage our readers to do the same. Resources are printed on recycled paper and more environmentally friendly groundwood papers (newsprint) whenever possible. The trees used are replaced through donations to the Scoutrees for Canada program. A portion of all profits is donated to charitable organizations.

Permissions

National Library of Canada Cataloguing in Publication
Main entry under title:
Creative worship 2: services for special days/compiled & edited by Ian Price.
 ISBN 1-55145-487-4
 1. Worship programs. 2. Church year. 3. Occasional services. I. Price, Ian, 1953-
BV25.C73 2003   264   C2003-910708-6

Published by Wood Lake Books Inc.
9025 Jim Bailey Road
Kelowna, British Columbia, Canada V4V 1R2
WEB: www.joinhands.com

Printing 10 9 8 7 6 5 4 3 2 1

Printed in Canada

Contents

# *Introduction*

GETTING STARTED & USING THIS RESOURCE

Creative Worship 2: Services for Special Days is the second worship resource in the *Creative Worship* series. Following *Creative Worship: Services from Advent to Pentecost,* we have become aware of the tremendous interest in creative worship for occasional use. Many congregations are embracing the vision of dynamic worship, especially relating to the key festivals of the Christian year, as well as other important occasions. We are also aware that many congregations are doing exciting and innovative things to bring worship fully alive, and to convey the truth of the gospel as relevantly as possible.

At the beginning of 2001, MediaCom and Wood Lake Books sought liturgies, litanies, and orders of worship from around Australia and Canada. Our hope was to gather some of the creative worship expressions being written and to offer them to the churches. *Creative Worship 2* is the result of that search. Many people responded, and we have selected those that best fit the criteria.

Those of us who are familiar with the previous publication will notice some variations this time round. First, because the material represents the work of people from very different situations, a decision needed to be made about the level of editing to apply to the original material. For the most part, we have decided to offer the material with as little editorial work as possible. This means that users will need to consider what is necessary at their end to make the material fit local needs. To this end, we have provided the material on disc, and ask that credit be given to the author and a statement "Used by permission of Wood Lake Books and Media-Com. All rights reserved" be printed on worship leaflets or bulletins.

It will also be necessary to consider appropriate music options where suggested songs are unknown locally. It is far easier for a local worship group to find known alternatives than for editors to go through the process of guessing what songs might be known across two continents.

These orders offer some startling possibilities for worship. In particular, there are a number of special liturgies such as A Christian Ritual Affirming Pregnancy; An Earth Day Service; A Service of Reconciliation for Congregations in Conflict; and A Service of Naming and Thanksgiving, that will spark the imagination of worship committees for all kinds of possibilities.

Worship is, quite possibly, the most important thing we do as Christians. Our prayer is that *Creative Worship 2* will be another catalyst for enriching the worship life of congregations around the world.

Ian Price

Gifts

Submitted by Rev. Kevin Little
Halifax, Nova Scotia, Canada

Introduction

This service could be adapted for use during any season, but is especially applicable for Advent – a time of waiting, seeking, and longing. At various points in the liturgy, participants are invited to reflect on various symbols that are made from clay. Sometimes the leader will shape the clay and reflect on it, at others, the participants are invited to shape their own piece of clay into one of the suggested symbols. So you will need quite a lot of clay!

There are opportunities for reflection. The leader will need to be sensitive to the progress of the participants, and above all, not rush them.

At the point of the offering, the children are invited to collect gifts and foodstuffs from the worshippers in pull-along wagons for distribution near to Christmas (or at another appropriate time, eg., Easter or Pentecost or church anniversary). People will need prior warning to bring gifts and foodstuff, and children invited to bring their wagons.

Greeting

The grace of the Lord Jesus Christ,
the love of God,
and the communion of the Holy Spirit
be with you all. (2 Corinthians 13:13)

Hymn   "Spirit of the Living God"

Opening Prayer

Loving God, we ask you to come among us and fill each and every one of us with your Spirit. We are each a unique vessel, open and ready to be filled, renewed, and reborn. Nurture us, feed us, and prepare us for your creative intentions. In the name of Jesus, who is our potter and our clay. Amen.

Distributing the Clay

Everyone receives a small amount of clay.

Fill Us	(a time of reflection)
	(The leader takes a large piece of clay and begins to mold it into a bowl, reflecting on the need to open ourselves to God in worship, in silence, in prayer. The worshippers are invited to adopt an open posture, hands outstretched, holding palms up, ready to receive. The clay is molded as a bowl, for a bowl needs to be filled – filled with the Spirit.)

Lighting of the Advent Wreath

The Word

First Lesson:	Isaiah 45, 64 (selected verses)
Hymn:	"O God Beyond All Face and Form" (*Voices United (VU)* # 304)
Gospel Lesson:	Luke 3:1–6

Molding the Clay

All are invited to mold the clay, using the following choice of symbols: candle, tree, candy cane, stocking, angel, bell, star, gift (box), ball (world).

Touch Us	(a time of reflection)
	(The leader takes pieces of clay and molds them into the various symbols, pausing after each to explain the significance of this gift to our Christian journey. God molds us, shapes us, takes our gifts and refines them for God's pleasure.)

The Response

Hymn:	"Abba! Father!"

Prayers of the People & Lord's Prayer

	One	Within our Christian family there are many different ways to pray. Some of us are quiet and reflective, some of us are busy and energetic, some like ritual, some like informality.
	Two	To me, a prayer is not a prayer unless it is spontaneous, from the heart.

Three	I don't care whether the prayer is an old prayer like "The Lord's Prayer" or "The Prayer of St. Francis," it has to have depth – meaning. Often, prayers said off the top of my head are repetitive, weak, and shallow. I need a prayer that speaks through the ages, one that has sustained Christians for generations.
One	So we invite you to pray with us and allow God to fill you, move you, and shape you into a new creation. Let us pray:
Two	Awesome and wonderful God, we raise our hands heavenward, turn our palms up to receive your Spirit, and look to you, drinking in the power of your love for us.
All	Thank you, Jesus.
	(Silence)
Three	Forgiving God, we bow down before you, our heads lowered, our eyes shut, our hearts heavy with the need of forgiveness. We are sorry for the sins we have committed, the pain we have caused, the good works not performed. We humbly ask for your forgiving grace.
All	Lord, hear our prayer, and in your love, answer.
	(Silence)
One	Glorious God, we are so thankful for the many blessings we have received from you. We stand now and take our neighbor's hand, connecting ourselves as your body in this community of faith. We are grateful for thankful hearts and joyful living. We are blessed to call this community home.
All	We love our neighbor as we love ourselves.
	(Silence)
Two	Healing God, we ask for your blessing upon those whose names rest on our hearts. As the Quakers have taught us, sometimes words get in the way of your message. So as we remain standing and holding each other's hands, we say the name of the person or persons who we pray for this morning. And as we say the name, we ask your healing touch to come upon our friend in Christ.
	(Silence)

One   O God, you are the great healer and physician.

All   Thanks be to God!

(Silence)

Three   Now we are bold to say the words our Lord taught us…

Our Father, who art in heaven...

Use Us   (a time of reflection)

(The leader asks the members of the congregation to consider with whom we would like to share the clay they have shaped. Perhaps a friend who is lonely could use the candy cane to pray to Jesus. Perhaps the bell to ring in some joy. Perhaps the star for some vision, or the angel for comfort, the Jesse Tree for roots, or the world for perspective, the stocking to remind us of St. Nicholas, etc... God uses our gifts to affect, touch, and inspire others.)

Offering of Gifts

"In the Bleak Midwinter"

(During the offering the children take their wagons and pull them down the aisle collecting the white gifts, the offering, the food bank stuffs.
People are invited to think of the time in the next week when they will deliver their clay gift to someone they know.)

Hymn: "Hark the Glad Sound"

Sung Dismissal and Blessing

"Go Now in Peace" (Shawnee Press Inc., Delaware Water Gap, PA)

or .

Dismissal and Blessing

Go now in peace,
to live in the grace of Christ
and the love of God,
shaped by the Spirit,
to live to the honor and glory of our Savior. Amen.

A Special Christmas Held During Advent

Submitted by
Rev. Dr. Sue Algate
Booval Qld 4304

Introduction

This service has been held with the involvement of adults and with the involvement of children.
An undecorated Christmas tree was placed in a central position.
A large symbol, and several small symbols of tinsel (or candles), angels, bells, shepherd crooks, stars and hearts were placed near the tree.
(These had been made by a person who enjoyed handicraft in the adult service, and by the children as part of their Sunday school activities in the family service. Several of each symbol were placed in baskets for distribution later.)

Choir: "A Christmas Blessing" (by Aubrey Podlich, *All Together Again*, # 194)

Carol: "Once in Royal David's City"

Prayer

Let us pray:
Loving God, we come with joy to worship you,
rejoicing that in Christ you became human and lived on this earth.

We love this Christmas season,
we know the story so well,
yet we get so busy with the many things that need to be done:
the gifts to purchase, wrap, and deliver;
the cards and letters that need to be written;
the food, the parties, the preparations for Christmas day –
so busy that we forget that your coming is central to all we do.

As we come now in this season of Advent,
remembering the story of your birth as we decorate our tree,
remind us of the love you have for us and for all people,
remind us of the reason for your coming among us,
kindle in us a deep desire to make room in our hearts and lives for you, and let us
sense again the wonder of your love and grace. Amen.

Comment on the Christmas tree

In Europe where Christmas was first celebrated, this time of the year is cold, often the ground is covered with snow, and most plant life dies, or at least loses its leaves until the coming of spring. The fir tree, an evergreen, is a reminder of God's constant love. God's love and grace is always available to us, even in the harshest of times. So as we come to decorate our tree, we do so remembering that the tree is symbolic of eternal life, and the constancy of God's love and presence.

Song: "O Tannenbaum"

Decorating the Christmas Tree

(As a person speaks of the significance of each of the decorations on the tree, the scripture is read, and another person decorates the tree with the relevant decorations.)

TINSEL

Tinsel is the equivalent of a string of candles or lights on the tree. Martin Luther, while walking home one clear Christmas Eve, was taken with the beauty of the stars twinkling through the fir trees. He wanted his children to appreciate this beauty and so he brought a fir tree into the house and added some candles as a reminder that Jesus is the light of the world. We continue to string tinsel, lights, and even some candle decorations onto our trees.

Bible Reading: John 1:1–5

Carol: "Silent Night"

ANGEL

Angels are very important in the Christmas story. The angel Gabriel came to Mary with the Good News that she would be the mother of this special child whom God had promised. An angel came to Joseph in a dream telling him that this child would be called Jesus, and that he is Emmanuel, which means "God with us." And on the night of Jesus' birth, the angels lit up the night sky singing praises to God. An angel is a messenger from God and we place angels on the tree as a reminder of the special role they played in the Christmas story.

Bible Reading: Luke 1:26–33

Carol: "Angels from the Realms of Glory" *(vss. 1 and 4)*

BELL

Bells are a symbol of joy, and Christmas has always been seen as a time of joy. When the angel appeared to the shepherds, they were told that the message of the birth of Jesus was one of great joy. When many others angels joined the first angel, they praised and gave glory to God.

Bible Reading: Luke 2:8–14

Carol: "Joy to the World"

SHEPHERDS' CROOK

The shepherds' crooks are a reminder of the shepherds and how they responded to the message of the angels. Because they spent all their time with their sheep they were unable to worship God with the rest of the Jewish people. For this reason they were looked down on. So it is so very special that these were the ones who were told the wonderful news of Jesus birth.

Bible Reading: Luke 2:15–18, 20

Carol: "The First Nowell" *(vss. 1–3)*

STAR

The stars on our trees are a reminder of the wise men who came such a long way to see Jesus because they had seen a special star in the sky and wanted to bring their worship and their gifts to this special child.

Bible Reading: Matthew 2:1–2, 9–10

In the time of King Herod, after Jesus was born in Bethlehem of Judea, sages from the East came to Jerusalem, asking, "Where is the child who has been born king of the Jews? For we observed his star at its rising, and have come to pay him homage."… Then they set out; and there, ahead of them, went the star that they had seen at its rising, until it stopped over the place where the child was. When they saw that the star had stopped, they were overwhelmed with joy.

Carol: "We Three Kings of Orient Are"

Offering:

As the offering is received the congregation sings the carol,
"As with Gladness" *(vss. 1-3)*

HEART

A heart is a symbol of love, and it's also a symbol of life. So we place hearts on the tree as a reminder of God's love for us, and that through Jesus we have the gift of abundant and eternal life. The heart also expresses our love for God and for each other.

Bible Reading: 1 John 4:7–12

Carol: "Away in a Manger"

Our Response:

We have decorated our tree,
remembering that the tree itself, an evergreen,
is a reminder that God's love is constant.
The tinsel recalls that Jesus is the light of the world;
the angel tells us of God's message of hope;
the bells remind us that this gift of God is one of great joy;
the shepherds' crooks declare that the message is for very ordinary people who
hear and respond to the Good News that Christ comes to bring peace on earth,
and to create goodwill;
the stars point to the Star of Bethlehem, once seen, its meaning perceived, and
followed until it brought the wise men to Jesus;
and the heart stands for the love of God, given to us in the birth of Christ.

As we look toward Christmas, what is it that we most need –
a reminder that Christ is the light who will show us the way,
the message of hope expressed by the angels,
joy,
the need to respond to what God has already spoken to our hearts and minds, expressed in the shepherd's crook,
the beckoning of the star to keep on following until we find where God is leading us,
or a heart that receives the love of God?

As the baskets of symbols come around the congregation, please choose one symbol – the one that you most need to keep in mind as you move now towards the celebration of Christmas. Take that symbol home, place it on your tree, and each time you see it, remember that Christ has come to meet you at your point of need.

The symbols are distributed

Please hold the symbol in your hand, as we come now in prayer.

Loving God,
thank you that this Advent season is the reminder of your coming amongst us.
Thank you that you are light in our darkness,
hope in times of despair,
joy in times of pain,
calling us, again, to respond to your leading,
showing us the way you would have us live,
and giving us the gift of your love.

In these coming days, as we look upon this symbol,
remind us that, by your coming,
you have reached out to affirm your love for us
and that you are ever willing to share the experiences of life with us.
Help us to receive the gift we most need this Christmas time,
for we pray it in your name. Amen.

Prayers for Others

Carol: "Hark the Herald Angels Sing" (*AHB* # 227)

Benediction Song: "A Christmas Blessing"

Communion with The Great I Am

A CHRISTMAS EVE EUCHARIST

Submitted by Jennifer and Ian Price
Rosefield Uniting Church Highgate S.A. Australia

Introduction

In the fourth gospel, John records a series of "I am…" statements of Jesus that reveal essential characteristics of the Christ. For Greek readers of the day, especially when accompanied by the word "true" or "real," these statements would be understood, against the Platonic idea of the perfect "type" residing in heaven, to point to the divinity of Christ.

For Hebrew readers, the same titles would evoke a memory of the name of God "I am who I am" (Exodus 3:14). In John 8:58, this link is reinforced by the statement of Jesus, "Before Abraham was, I am."

So these titles point us to some special characteristics of the nature of Jesus as the Christ, characteristics that shape the nature of faith, and the nature of the Christian community. Those who are disciples live out these truths, and seek to follow the pattern of these ways.

In this service of worship, best celebrated with holy communion at or near midnight, we enter into the mystery of the Christ, the incarnation of God, seeking to be renewed, restored and sent into the world in service.

Call to Worship

Narrator   Jesus said, "Very truly I tell you, I am the gate for the sheep… Whoever enters by me will be saved, and will come in and go out and find pasture." (John 10:7, 9)

Singing Group: "You are Mine" (by David Haas in *As One Voice* Vol 2 # 2)

Leader   Christ calls us here – to this time and place.
The way is open for us to enter into communion with God.
We come to celebrate, to hear the call of Jesus,
and to discover our place in creation.

All   Move among us here, we pray.
Touch us with your Spirit.

Heal the hurt we bear.
Move us to compassion.
Give us courage for the journey.

Leader   Let us worship the living God,
the one born among us.

All   Let us worship the Christ, and enter into the mystery of faith.

Carols: "O Little Town of Bethlehem"
"Once in Royal David's City"

Narrator   Jesus said, "I am the good shepherd.
The good shepherd lays down his life for the sheep…
I know my own and my own know me,
just as the Father knows me and I know the Father.
And I lay down my life for the sheep…"
(John 10:11, 14, 15)

Prayer of Confession

Leader   Let us reflect on our relationship with God
and the quality of our living.
Loving God,
you come to us in the person of Jesus,
showing us the way to live.

All   Remind us who and whose we are.

(Silent reflection)

Leader   You invite us to share in your ministry and mission in the world.
You give us words to speak.
You lead us into the places of pain and suffering to bring healing.
You equip us for service.

All   Forgive us, we pray, for being slow to speak the truth,
for being apathetic in the face of suffering,
and silent in speaking out against injustice.

(Silent reflection)

Leader	You gave your life, that we might have life. You embraced us, even when we did not deserve it.
All	Renew in us a right Spirit. Restore us in your likeness. Free us, we pray, from all that mars your purpose in us.
	(Silent reflection)

Assurance of Forgiveness

Narrator	Jesus said, "My sheep hear my voice. I know them, and they follow me. I give them eternal life, and they will never perish." (John 10:27–28)
Leader	By the grace of Christ and the love of God, we are set free.
All	Thanks be to God. Amen.
	(The Christ Candle is lit.)
Narrator	Jesus said, "I am the light of the world. Whoever follows me will never walk in darkness but have the light of life." (John 8:12)
Leader	Just as the flower does not bloom without the gentle warmth and light of the sun, so we need the light of Christ to bring us to fullness of life.
All	Shine upon our darkness. Bring forth beauty in all colors and hues. Lighten our paths and show us your way.

Carols:	"Silent Night, Holy Night" "The First Nowell"
Narrator	Jesus said, "I am the way, and the truth, and the life. No one comes to the Father except through me. If you know me, you will know my Father also. From now on you do know him and have seen him." (John 14:6–7)

Bible Reading:	John 1:1–5, 10–14
	Luke 2:8–14

Singing Group: "O Holy Night" (by J.S. Dwight)

Address

Carols: "Born in the Night, Mary's Child"
"Infant Holy"

Offering

Narrator   Jesus said, "Very truly, I tell you,
the one who believes in me will also do the works that I do
and in fact, will do, greater works than these,
because I am going to the Father." (John 14:12)

All: Let the gifts that we offer this night speak of our love
for you and all people.

(The offering is received)

Leader   Receive the gifts we bring.

All   May they be gifts of life.

Leader   Receive the offerings of our hearts.

All   May they be gifts of love.

Leader   Receive the longings of our Spirits.

All   May they be gifts of light. Amen.

Singing Group: "Peace Child" (by Shirley Murray in *Carol our Christmas* # 35)

Memorial Moment

Narrator   Jesus said, "I am the resurrection and the life.
Those who believe in me, even though they die,
will live, and everyone who believes in me will never die."
(John 11:25, 26)

Leader   Let us remember all for whom this night is touched with sadness
because of the loss of a loved one;
because of the heartache and horror of the world's violence;
because of an unfulfilled longing;
because of pain and suffering.

All   O God, let your grace, mercy, and peace flow through the earth,
to heal,
to save,
and to bring hope for all.

Leader   Let us light candles of hope in the name of the Christ.

(The people are invited to come forward and light candles and
spend a time in personal prayer.)

Singing Group: "Justice in the Womb" (by John L. Bell, *Innkeepers & Light
Sleepers* # 28)

Narrator   "The light shines in the darkness,
and the darkness did not overcome it." (John 1:5)

Holy Communion

Narrator   Jesus said, "I am the bread of life.
Whoever comes to me will never me hungry,
and whoever believes in me will never be thirsty…
I am the living bread that came down from heaven.
Whoever eats this bread will live forever;
and the bread that I will give for the life of the world
is my flesh." (John 6:35, 51)

Leader   In the desert, our ancestors were fed the manna.

All   You fed them and they were satisfied.
Thanks be to God, who feeds the hungry and meets every
need.

Narrator	Jesus said, "Those who drink of the water that I will give will never be thirsty. The water that I will give will become in them a spring of water gushing up to eternal life… Let anyone who is thirsty come to me, and let the one who believes in me drink… I am the true vine…" (John 4:14; 7:37, 38; 15:1)
Leader	In the desert, our ancestors drank water from the rock.
All	They drank and their thirst was quenched. Thanks be to God, who satisfies every need.
Narrator	On the night of his betrayal, Jesus took a loaf of bread, and after blessing it he broke it, gave it to the disciples, and said, "Take, eat; this is my body." Then he took a cup, and after giving thanks he gave it to them, saying, "Drink from it all of you; for this is my blood of the new covenant, which is poured out for many for the forgiveness of sins. I tell you, I will never again drink of this fruit of the vine until that day when I drink it with you in my Father's kingdom." (Matthew 26:26–29)
Leader	The bread of heaven is broken for us.
All	We shall feed on the food of eternal life.
Leader	The cup of salvation is given for us.
All	The gift of eternal life given for all.
Leader	The peace of God be with you.
All	And also with you.
	(Signs of peace are exchanged.)
Leader	We break this bread in the name of Christ.
All	We shall feed upon the bread of life.

Leader	We raise this cup, sign of covenant grace.
All	We shall drink and be satisfied.
	(Holy Communion is shared)

Blessing

May Christ, the light of the world, dwell in you.
May Christ, the good shepherd, keep you safe.
May Christ, the way the truth and life, lead you on.
And may Christ, the resurrection and the life, bring you home.

Carol: "O Come All Ye Faithful"

(During the singing of the carol, candles are lit from the Christ candle and shared from person to person throughout the congregation until the church is ablaze with light.)

Leader	Let us take our light into the world for all to see.
All	Let our light shine forever to the glory of God.
Leader	Amen.
All	Amen!

Postlude (sung) "The Carol of the Bells" (Peter J. Wilhausky)

Palm Sunday

Submitted by Rev. Lorraine Covington,
Westmeadows, Victoria

Introduction

This service was inspired by a need to refocus on the events of Palm Sunday leading into the passion of Holy Week. Good Friday's liturgy often seems to be a re-read of Palm Sunday's gospel. Some people turn off with a sense of, "I've heard all this before."

In this service, the focus is on a series of simple overhead projector transparencies depicting aspects of the story. They are accompanied by readings and silences to allow the worshippers to bring their own identity and recollections to the familiar story. For this reason, it may be best to have the passages read from the back of the worship gathering, to highlight the meditative aspect of the worship.

Making and distributing crosses made from palm leaves, and decorating the sanctuary with palm branches, enhance the sense of the occasion. The crosses may be given to worshippers as they come forward to receive the communion elements, and can be held aloft during the singing of the last hymn.

Welcome

Introduction to the Service

Explain that there will be periods of silence, as aspects of the Palm Sunday narrative are depicted.

Opening Prayer

Awaken me to your presence;
alert me to your love;
affirm me in your peace;
open me to your way to walk in humility and justice;
enfold me in your light, that I may share your journey;
for my heart is ready, Lord, my heart is ready.

First Overhead   (Jesus entering Jerusalem on donkey)

Silent Reflection

Reading: Matthew 21:1–11
(Use a second person for a voice-over prophet verse 5)

Song:	"Hosanna Hosanna" (*Songs of the Vineyard* # 29)
Peace (together)	Blessed is he who comes in the name of the Lord and brings his peace to share.
	Priest/leader: Peace be with you.
	Response: And also with you.
Second Overhead	(Judas' betrayal for 30 pieces of silver)
Silent Reflection	
Reading:	Matthew 26:14–16

Prayer of Confession

Lord of the passion, our light and living water,
come and restore us.
Dispel the darkness in our lives.
Destroy the self-centeredness that leads us to brokenness.
Defeat within us, our denial of your love.
Enter our darkrooms of guilt and shame,
the secret places of our sin – hidden and unforgiven.
Come, Lord of light, and forgive us.
Come, Lord of living water – cleanse and refresh us.
Come and scatter our darkness,
draw us to the light of your eternal life.

(Silence)

Absolution	God of light and passion, restore you to the fullness of life, forgive your sins and empower you to live anew in his strength, through Jesus Christ our Savior. Amen.
Hymn:	"My Song is Love Unknown"
Homily	
Third Overhead	(The Last Supper)
Silent Reflection	
Reading:	Luke 22:14–21

Hymn:	"An Upper Room Did Our Lord Prepare"

Prayers of the People

Invite worshippers to name individuals, world situations, and local issues. As each person names a situation, invite the people to respond,

Grant your peace, O Christ.

Fourth Overhead	(Peter's Denial)

Silent Reflection

Readings:	Prediction: Luke 22:31–34
	Denial: Luke 22:54–62

Hymn:	"Were You There when They Crucified Our Lord"

Fifth Overhead	(Jesus tortured)

Silent Reflection

Reading:	Matthew 27:27-31

Hymn:	"And Now O Father Mindful of Thy Love"

Offertory

Liturgy for Holy Communion (according to local custom)

During the reception of communion, the congregation is invited to join in the Taizé chant, "Jesus remember me when I come into your kingdom."

Palm crosses are distributed as individuals come forward for the reception of the holy sacrament of communion.

Hymn:	"Lift High the Cross"
	(Process out at last two verses, holding palm crosses high and aloft.)

Liturgy for Palm Sunday

PALM SUNDAY

Submitted by Mrs. Annette Kearse
Morningside, Queensland

This service centers around a dramatic presentation called "Why are you here?"
It is in the form of an interview.

You will need a portable microphone.
The people taking part need to be "placed" on one side of the sanctuary.
The assistant priests and the last character to be interviewed need to be a little distance away from the other characters.

Opening Sentence

So Jesus came, riding on a donkey.
Hosanna! Hosanna!

Hymn Choose from:

"Ride On, Ride On in Majesty"
"Make Way, Make Way" (*Complete Mission Praise (CMP)* #457)
"Children of Jerusalem" (*CMP* #70)
"We cry, Hosanna, Lord" (*CMP* #725)

Introduction

Come with us, as we explore Palm Sunday, the beginning of Holy Week – a week which should be imprinted on our minds and hearts, because of the great love shown to us by Jesus Christ.

Reader

Have you ever wondered who the people were who joined in to welcome Jesus into the city of Jerusalem?
Why were they there?
Were they curious, had they seen him before, had he done some marvellous thing for them?
Come with us and find out!

WHY ARE YOU HERE?

Newsreader	This is the Jerusalem News. There has been a report of a heavy crowd of people lining the city streets. In some places they are up to four people deep. Our roving reporter Benjamin is out there… Benjamin can you tell us why these crowds have gathered?
Benjamin	Hello there, Paul. As I speak, people are still arriving. I hope to find out why they are here? (Turns to person standing near him) Sir, can you tell me why you are here?
Curious person	My friend told me about this man. He'd heard him talk to a group down by the lake. His words were challenging – love your enemies, do good to those who hate you. To me, it seems unusual to say love your enemies – it's natural to hate – easier too! So I'm curious; that's why I am here!
Benjamin	Thank you! A person who says love your enemy – I'd say that was extremely challenging. (Turns to a woman with a child) Ma'am, can you tell me why you are here?
Woman	A group of us took our children to see this man. His friends told us to go away, not to disturb him – but this man said, "Let the children come to me." He took them on his lap, and blessed them. To him, children are precious. That's why we are here.
Benjamin	Thank you, Ma'am! A man who speaks challenging words and thinks children are precious. I wonder who he is?
Child	Sir! Sir! I can tell you who he is?

Benjamin	You can! Who is he?
Child	It's Jesus! Jesus!
Other children nearby	
	Yes, it's Jesus, Jesus, Jesus.
Benjamin	Jesus! The name sounds familiar.
	(Turns to child)
	Did he really put you on his knee and bless you?
Child	Yes he did. Jesus is such a kind person.
Benjamin	Thank you. (turns to another person) Can you tell me why you are here?
Blind man	You ask me why I am here! I'll tell you why. He healed me! I was blind. I had to beg for a living. One day he visited Jericho where I lived. I cried out to him, "Take pity on me!" Those around me told me to be quiet, but I still cried out and he heard me. He asked me what I wanted and I told him. I will never forget his words. "Then see, your faith has made you well." That is why I am here.
Benjamin	That is amazing! Thank you for telling your story. Paul, are you there?
Newsreader (Paul)	
	I'm here, Benjamin. Have you found the reason for the large crowds?
Benjamin	Yes, Paul. It is Jesus who is coming. Jesus who spoke challenging words. Who thinks children are precious and who heals people.
Newsreader	Jesus – the name is familiar. We will search to see if he is on our files. In the meantime, keep on interviewing!

Benjamin	Okay, Paul. Now let's see. Those two over there look interesting.
	By the look of their clothes they must be from the Temple.
	Sir, can you tell me why you are here?
Annas	I am Annas. I am an assistant to the High Priest at the Temple.
	We have heard disturbing reports about this Jesus.
	We heard that he talks about religious matters to the common people. I tell you that all religious matters are dealt with by the church officials and not by any itinerant preacher.
Levi	That's right! This Jesus teaches that the Kingdom of God is here and that we must love our enemies.
	Love our enemies!! Hate them, use them – but love them!?
	I ask you!
Benjamin	Yes, I heard about loving your enemies but surely that is a…
Annas	Do you know he said that, "The Father and I are one"!
	BLASPHEMY! NO ONE can be the same as God.
	Yes, we are keeping our eye on this man Jesus.
Levi	WE certainly are. YOU make sure, young man, that you don't get caught up with this Jesus' teachings.
Benjamin	I can see why the established church would be worried.
	Thank you for giving me your reasons.
	Phew! They did get rather heated!
	Now, I wonder who that is, sulking behind that pillar.
	(Approaches pillar and speaks to the man)
	Sir, can you tell me why you are here?
Man	Sssh! Over here! I'm here to see if this Jesus could be the man we need to lead us against the R's.
Benjamin	The R's?
Man	YES, the R's, you know – those who rule us.

Benjamin	Oh! Them! The R's!
Man	We want to see if Jesus will help us rout the R's once and for all!
Benjamin	I see. You are talking insurrection, rebellion.
Man	That's right! Now go away!
Benjamin	Paul, are you there Paul?
Newsreader	Hello, Benjamin, what else have you discovered?
Benjamin	Only that there are many people from different walks of life who want to see Jesus – some because he heals, loves children, and speaks challenging words. He appears to be a loving sort of person. However, there are those who find Jesus disturbing. The church officials say he has committed blasphemy. Others have, shall we say, political reasons for looking to him. I, for one, will be curious to see this Jesus. Over to you, Paul.
Newsreader	Thank you, Benjamin. This Jesus sounds like a fascinating man. We must keep an eye on further developments. And now the news from Bethany. It appears that a very expensive perfume has been wasted… (fades out)
Reader	So there we have it. So many people wanting to see Jesus. Some very happy even to the point of becoming followers. Others intent on condemning him for his words and actions. Some watching to see if he could be their leader. What will Jesus mean to you?

Hymn: "Lord of the Dance"

Prayers of Thanksgiving

Gracious God, as we celebrate the coming of our Savior,
remembering all he said and did,
we bring our prayers for others, believing in your Spirit's power to speak words of
grace, and bring healing and hope.

Loving Jesus,
you came bringing love. May we, your followers, show
love to others.
May we hold out the hand of friendship to all who need
encouragement, who are ill, who are lonely.

Lord, be our guide.

Lord Jesus,
you came bringing peace. May we be peacemakers in a
world where hatred and hostility prevail.
Help us to show a new way of living with others.

Lord, be our guide.

Lord Jesus,
we come bringing joy. Enable us to show what joy really
means, born of the knowledge that someone cares, that
we are never alone. We believe there is always someone
willing to listen, and that someone is you, O Lord.

Lord, be our guide.

Be ever present in our lives and may we always be aware
of you.
Hear us as we remember in silence those for whom we
have concern this day.

(Silent prayer)

In faith we have offered our prayers.
In faith we look to you to answer them.
In faith we seek to be your servants.

Lord, be our guide. Amen.

Greeting of the Peace

Let us greet one another in the love of Christ with the words:

The grace and peace of God be always with you.

Hymn: Choose from:

"On a Hill Far Away" (*CMP* #536)
"There is a Green Hill" (*CMP* #674)
"There is a Redeemer" (*CMP* #673)
"Come, see the Beauty of the Lord" (*CMP* #100)

The Great Thanksgiving

From the beginning
You have loved us
From the beginning
You created us
From the beginning
You have shown us the way.
Therefore, in gratitude
We bring our thanks
For your sacrifice on the cross.
Your sacrifice
that bought our redemption.
Therefore, we lift our voices and proclaim
Glory, Glory, Glory,
may our praises inhabit your Kingdom.

Your body
broken
disfigured
suffering pain
humiliation.
Your body
our bread
broken for us.
Come
take, eat
be restored.
Your blood
our wine
given freely for us.
Take
drink
receive new life.

In doing so, become one
with my body.
One body
You and I
giving, sharing, loving
bringing new life to all.

Come, share in his love given freely for you.

The Elements are Shared

Dismissal

Give thanks to the Lord
all you people
give him thanks.
For it is the Lord
that brings peace and joy,
forgiveness and hope.
It is the Lord who gives
strength and courage
to do our daily work.

Lord, we thank you.
We offer ourselves
to be your agents
in this your hurting world.
In your power we go forth.
Amen.

Hymn Choose from:

"The Lord is Marching out in Splendour" (*Ring of Praise* # 103)
"Come On and Celebrate" (*CMP* # 99)
"Jesus Is Lord! Creation's Voice Proclaims It."(*CMP* # 367)
"Ride On, Ride On"
"There is a Green Hill"

Benediction

Let us go to seek the presence of Christ;
to share the love of God;
and obey the call of the Spirit. Amen.

The Bread of Life:

A LITURGY FOR MAUNDY THURSDAY, INCORPORATING A SHARED MEAL AND COMMUNION SERVICE

Submitted by Rev. Sharla Hulsey and Mrs. Duretta Quail
First Christian Church (Disciples of Christ) Sac City, IO, USA

Introduction

In the Christian Church (Disciples of Christ), Maundy Thursday is traditionally the celebration of the institution of the Lord's supper (eucharist or communion). Some congregations observe a Passover seder, pointing toward the origins of communion in a passover meal. Others have tried creative approaches, including a simulated early Christian catacomb service, drama, or other such liturgy.

This year at the First Christian Church in Sac City, Iowa, we decided to combine the traditional potluck meal with the worship service. The theme for the evening was "The Bread of Life." The original liturgy below is the one we used that evening.

In preparation for the service, I suggested having a few members gifted in baking make several different kinds of bread (we had corn bread, baking powder biscuits, sourdough rolls, dark rye bread, and Irish soda bread; we purchased a box of matzot for the communion bread). The rest of the participants should bring something to share that can be passed around the table (we asked for hors d'oeuvres and finger foods, and – in a real-life illustration of the scripture at hand – no one went away hungry).

The entire service takes place at the dinner table. If at all possible, the worship space should be arranged so all participants can sit around one table, such as a number of folding tables arranged in a square with people sitting only on the outside. The communion elements should be in the centre of one end of the table. Keep table decorations simple: plain white tablecloths and votive candles in clear holders are adequate.

Since there are six places in the liturgy for breaking bread (including the communion bread), place the different kinds of bread in baskets at reasonably regular intervals around the table. Have someone designated to read each scripture passage and seat them within reach of each basket of bread. After five readings and breakings of bread, with five responses of the Taizé chorus "Eat This Bread," participants are invited to share the meal. When people are mostly finished eating, call them back to worship through the singing (solo or ensemble/choir) of "Break Thou the Bread of Life," and move into the communion service.

Since my congregation was not familiar with the Taizé chorus used here, we had a solo voice sing it once at each reading and then had the congregation repeat it once. If the congregation already knows it, the solo voice can be omitted.

The hymns used in this service are in the Christian Church (Disciples of Christ) hymnal, Chalice Hymnal (St. Louis, MO, USA: Chalice Press, 1995) but are no doubt available in other sources. All scriptures are from the New Revised Standard Version.

Gathering and Preparing for Worship

Call to Worship "All Who Hunger, Gather Gladly" (vocal solo or ensemble/choir)

Greeting and Statement of Purpose

Prayer of Invocation and Blessing (in unison)
> Blessed are you, Lord our God, ruler of the universe,
> for you satisfy the hungry in body and spirit.
> You fed your children, the Israelites, with manna and quail,
> and sustained them by your presence
> as they wandered in the wilderness.
> You have been faithful to your children throughout history,
> and we have not wanted for sustenance.
> Bless us now, O Lord, we pray:
> bless this meal we share;
> meet us in bread, and drink,
> through your written and spoken Word,
> and in this company of disciples.
> Bind us together into one body
> as we share one bread
> and remember the one Lord of all,
> your Son, Jesus the Christ,
> in whose name we pray. Amen.

Response: "We Come as Guests Invited" (verse 1)

Hearing God's Word

Scripture Reading: John 6:1–14 and breaking of the first bread

Response: "Eat This Bread" (a cappella or accompanied; solo voice once, then congregation repeats) (*Chalice Hymnal*, # 386.)

Scripture Reading: John 6:16–27 and breaking of the second bread

Response: "Eat This Bread" (as before)

Scripture Reading: John 6:28–34 and breaking of the third bread

Response: "Eat This Bread" (as before)

Scripture Reading: John 6:35–40 and breaking of the fourth bread

Response: "Eat This Bread" (as before)

Scripture Reading: John 6:41–51 and breaking of the fifth bread

Response: "Eat This Bread" (as before)

Sharing the Meal (pass potluck items around the table)

Remembering the Last Supper

Musical Meditation: "Break Thou the Bread of Life" (solo or ensemble/choir)

Scripture Reading: Luke 22:1–20 and breaking of the sixth (communion) bread, and pouring of the cup

Musical Meditation: "Now the Silence, Now the Peace" (solo)

Distribution of the Elements

As we partake, join in singing "Eat This Bread" as a meditation.

The celebrant, who broke the bread, serves the person to his/her right, who then serves the person to his/her right, and so on around the table until everyone has received the elements. (This works well when done by intinction.)

Prayer of Thanksgiving (in unison)

Blessed are you, Lord our God, ruler of the universe.
You have taken what we have offered here
and turned it into abundance,
nourishing our bodies and our spirits.
You have fed us with your Son, Jesus Christ,
the Bread of Life,
and surpassed even your own love and generosity
shown to your people in the wilderness.
Help us to remember what you have done here tonight,
and what you have been doing
since the dawn of creation:
nourishing us and giving us life.
Help us ever to be thankful. Amen.

Response: "One Bread, One Body" (chorus only)
Dismissal

Go in peace.
Let the suffering of the Christ set you free.
Let the blessing of the Spirit bring you life.
Let the love of God make you whole.
Go in peace.

Pentecost Worship

TOUCHED BY FIRE

Submitted by Rev. Terry Shillington
Mckillop, Alberta, Canada

Call to Worship

Come, with your celebrations and joys.
Come, with your dreams for the church of Jesus Christ.
Prepare to enter into God's dream for us.

We come,
to offer up the gifts of our lives,
and to receive the power of the Spirit in our lives.

Prayers of Approach

O God, who calls us and waits for us to come home,
we would bring the real stuff of our lives to offer in worship.
We long to be touched and filled with your Spirit,
for we come in hunger and waiting.
Surprise us and fill us as we worship.
We pray in the name of Jesus,
the Christ. Amen.

Hymn:

"Holy Spirit Hear Us"

Prayers of Reconciliation

Gracious God, Loving Host, even before we knew you,
you invited us in and made us welcome.

Before we had opened our hearts and learned to love,
you had opened your heart to us.

We confess eyes often closed to encountering you,
in our brothers and sisters,
in your people, so different from us.
We pray, open our eyes.

We confess hearts often closed to compassion,
when our brothers and sisters know a different truth,
when our own standards and values are offended.
We pray, open our hearts.

We confess our spirits often closed to your Spirit,
for you invite us into an adventure of faith;
you would knock down our own walls
and teach us new languages of prayer and faith.
We pray that you will open our spirits to your Spirit.

O Loving Host for all the people of God,
warm us in your hospitality and surround us in your persistent, welcoming grace.
Amen.

Words of Assurance

Enter into the good news of Jesus Christ.
Let the Holy Spirit fill us afresh,
that we may let go of the darkness
and walk forever in peace.

Anthem: "Soon and Very Soon"

Listening for God's Word:
                      Acts 2:1–21

Hymn: "Open My Eyes"

Play: *Touched by Fire* (page 50)

Responding with our Lives

Hymn: "She Flies On"

The Ministry of the People

Offering

Offertory Hymn: "Though I May Speak"

Prayers of the People

Gracious God, we come before you – a people of saints and sinners, of humor, passion and pain.
We pray that the Holy Spirit may touch our congregations and leaders again with tongues of fire,
with the wind of the Spirit blowing through our meetings,
our worship,
and our living in the world.

We think of tiny rural and isolated congregations.
May you bless them with new creativity and energy,
as they seek ways to be healthy and spirit-filled.

We remember congregations challenged by change and the need to change.
Give us bold vision, blended with gracious respect for one another.

Bless us with a bold evangelical spirit,
where we are quiet and timid about speaking our faith.

Grant us hope and new excitement when we despair,
forgetting you are a maker of miracles among us.
Let us grow to be the gospel church our mothers and fathers dreamed of, that day long ago. May we be the church you dream for us!
Amen and Amen!

Hymn: "Spirit, Spirit of Gentleness"

Commissioning

Go, and let the Spirit blow through your life.
Go, and may the fire of faith be in you.
Go, in the love God,
as followers of Jesus Christ.

Touched by Fire

A PLAY

Time required for this drama – 22 min.

Introduction   This somewhat whimsical drama in the images of Pentecost invites us back to the fundamentals of that first Pentecost. We are called back to be an outreaching church that tells our story to the world – and tells it with fire and passion.

Characters   Narrator (can be one of the actors)
Rev. Folded Hands, a clergyman
Jenny Sameway, and Harry Von Dont Rok de Bote   (Traditionalists)
Annie Fixtheworld (a social activist)
Betty Busy Feet (a youth worker)
Mrs. Many Meetings (a church woman)
Cindi E.Z. Bord (a teenager)
(plus several of her friends)
Bill Kool   (a fringe observer and seeker)
The Prophet (perhaps a woman)

Props   • a Bible for Rev. Folded Hands
• Jenny & Harry – formally dressed
• a lengthy petition for Annie Fixtheworld
• Betty – roller blades over shoulder
• Mrs. Many Meetings – a little date book
• Cindi E.Z. Bord and her friends have Walkman sets on their heads
• Bill Kool – a golf putter and sunglasses
• The Prophet – wears a loose flowing gown and shawl (preferably red)
• a candle on the communion table
• small table by the prophet's chair, with a red cloth
• A basket of red stick candles (one for each of the characters in the drama)

NOTE: Concerning the movement of people in this drama.
At the beginning the actors might sit in the front pew of the church (on both sides), so that they come out of the congregation, and approach the prophet alternately from the left and the right. A microphone on each side of the prophet will suffice. As they leave centre stage (after consulting with the prophet), they might all move to one side of the platform, so that they are close and can quickly reassemble around the candle, when the prophet summons them for the closing.

Touched by Fire

Narrator

This drama in the images of Pentecost invites us back to the fundamentals of that first Pentecost. We are called back to be an outreaching church that tells our story to the world – and tells it with fire and passion.

As the drama unfolds we meet some very ordinary people, who sound like the folks of our own church. As they approach the prophet, we can laugh at them, and at ourselves. We can see ourselves and the challenge we need to hear for ourselves. Threaded through the dialogue is the central theme – that we are called to be a people in mission, turned outward; that success for us is deep, transforming faith that flows into outreach, not statistics, nor programs and accomplishments.

Prophet

(Standing, or walking in center of platform)

Fire – it leaps and dances,
it warms the cold and
nudges the unmoving to action.

Wherever the risen Christ is among us,
look for fire.
Look for tongues of flames reaching out
to touch Christians with lively faith,
and a spirit of hope.

Whenever this risen Christ is among us,
look for tongues of flames
reaching out from Christians,
from the church,
touching a cynical, unbelieving world.

Look for fire in a church
that is marked by the Spirit of Jesus Christ.

I am the prophet. I live among the people. I point the way to the
Spirit of Jesus Christ, who moves among us. I help the people
listen to the wisdom of God.
Over the ages I've been in bishops and moderators, in hymn writers and poets.
I have encouraged ordinary Christians to be open and faithful over the ages.
Today we listen for the Spirit's presence in your church.

(Sits down in a regal chair – angled partly away from congregation)

(Enter Rev. Folded Hands)

Rev F.H.   Hello! My name is Rev. James Folded Hands.
              I am the minister of St. Big & Bustling United Church down the way...
              Well, at least we'd like to be big and bustling....
              But we're always short of money! And some of us are rather tired.

Prophet   Hello, Reverend. Do you come seeking some help?

Rev   I want to see my church thrive. I pray about it.
              I go to a lot of meetings. I work hard on my sermons.
              I do my continuing education faithfully.
              (Holding hand on chest pompously.)
              I live a spotless life.

Prophet   Sounds good so far.

Rev   Then, too, our church is very up-to-date.
              We have marvelous graphics in our Sunday folder.
              We use the latest computer.
              Lately, we put in a new phone system.
              But the church is not full, and sometimes my people
              get downright cranky with one another.
              I think something is missing.

Prophet   What is it that God wants from your church?
              What kind of a church are you called to be?

Rev   I want it to be thriving, pews full, choirs singing marvelous
              anthems, lots of people in Bible study.

Prophet   But what do you suppose God's dream is – for you, and your
              people?

Rev   I am sure it is to fill the church, with all the bills paid.
              Doesn't it say that in 2 Corinthians somewhere?

Prophet   How is it to grow full?

Rev   I don't know. We have greeters at the door for newcomers.
              And nice blue cards to fill out.

Prophet	But how do you tell people about your faith?
Rev	Well, we have a church ad – costs us almost 2,000 bucks a year!
Prophet	But do you speak of your faith in your words and deeds?
Rev	Oh probably. We have a nice parking lot too! With three spaces for visitors (holding up three fingers). What more do we need?
Prophet	(compassionately) You need the fire of the Spirit in your leading, in your own worship. You might ask for the wind of the Spirit to blow through your groups, moving you to look out into the world.
Rev	Oh??? Right! (reluctantly)
	(Prophet holds hand out in blessing as Rev. Folded Hands walks away.)

	(Enter Jenny Sameway & Harry Von Dont Rok de Bote)
Jenny	Hello, I'm Jenny Sameway.
Harry	Yes, and I'm Harry Von Dont Rok de Bote.
Prophet	Welcome to the prophet's place! What do you seek?
Jenny	We need help with our church. It seems to be getting seriously off the rails.
Prophet	That sounds pretty serious!
Jenny	Yes it is. We need to get more young people involved.
Prophet	I'm sure that's part of God's dream for your church too.
Harry	Yes, we like kids and youth. Mind you, we like them to sit quietly and behave themselves. And they should be properly dressed.

Jenny	Yes, we want them to learn the good old hymns and to love communion the way we do. We'd like to get them ready to take our place on the committees. You know, we're not as young as we used to be.
Prophet	How is the Spirit of Jesus Christ filling you and changing you?
Jenny	(Startled) What has that to do with this? Well, now that you mention it, the Holy Spirit helps us make our budget, and to find new committee members when people move away.
Prophet	Anything else?
Harry	Well, I wish the Spirit would move people to give more – and to attend more regularly. And you know, we don't need all these changes some of these new ministers insist on. We don't need this new music. We need to learn the good old hymns!
Jenny	We shouldn't be upsetting so many people either. We're not supposed to be hugging in church.
Harry	Yes, and clapping!!
Jenny	And male ministers really need to be in charge. People respond better to a man!
Prophet	I can see why you are upset.
Jenny	Yes, and people don't want to be upset in church. They need peace and quiet, after a stressful week.
Prophet	Where is the Spirit leading you in all this?
Harry	I'm sure the Spirit is leading us to recover the good old ways of faith... ...I'm sure!
Prophet	(Compassionately) I believe the fire of the Spirit would touch your certainties and your contentment, and burn them away. The wind of the Holy Spirit might give you courage to change as the world has changed.

This fire and wind might move you to reach out to a new generation, to those who don't understand the good old ways.

Jenny	(To Harry as they move away) She has her nerve!

(Prophet holds hand out in blessing.)

(Enter Annie Fixtheworld)

Prophet	Welcome to my place! And you are??
Annie	I'm Annie Fixtheworld. I was hoping to get your signature.
Prophet	Annie, you look out of breath!
Annie	Right now, I have a petition and I'm getting signatures – you know, concerning the Upper Smolgarian issue.
Prophet	The Upper Smolgarian issue?
Annie	Do you know the people on the south side of the Bongo River in Upper Smolgaria are suffering from water pollution – from Canadian manufacturing plants in Upper Smolgaria. And the Canadian government is doing nothing about it!
Prophet	You're pretty passionate about this.
Annie	It's God's will that all people should know justice – and health!
Prophet	True! What are you doing to touch people right around you?
Annie	I'm recycling all paper. I have a petition to the city council to expand recycling options.
Prophet	But Annie, has the fire of the Spirit warmed your heart?
Annie	O yes, I'm pushing the janitor to get rid of all noxious chemicals.
Prophet	Has your own life been transformed by the Spirit?

Annie	Why certainly. I'm now eating tofu. And I brought veggie burgers to the church picnic.
Prophet	(Compassionately) Annie, may the fire of the Spirit touch you, so this gospel of Jesus Christ touches you deep in your own heart where your own fears and hopes are. May the wind of the Spirit blow through your caring and your wonderful causes, so that you are known as a lover too. (Prophet holds hand out in blessing, as Annie exits to the side.)

(Betty Busy Feet comes hurrying up to the platform.)

Betty	Hi, I'm Betty Busy Feet, the youth worker for this church. I'm in quite a rush. Do you have a minute?
Prophet	Why yes! What is it you are busy with, Betty?
Betty	Well, I have a lot of programs. Every Sunday evening I have a fun-night with the kids. We listen to music, play games, and of course eat. Then once a month, we have a FUN-FUN-FUN-FUN weekend. We bring lots of food. We don't have too much in the way of structure. We just go the way the Spirit leads us.
Prophet	Does the Spirit lead you?
Betty	O yes, we have a great time. Mind you, the Spirit leads some to go off in the dark together – and to do some things – well I won't go there. I have to be vigilant all the time.
Prophet	Is faith growing in your people?
Betty	I think so. They never like to talk about these things. It makes them uncomfortable. I wait till they bring it up.
Prophet	How does the Spirit of Jesus Christ shape and change your young people?
Betty	Well, we talk about sex regularly. Does that count? You know – about dating and parents too.

Prophet	Do you have a mission?
Betty	Well, let me see. Last year we had a car wash project.
Prophet	And what was the purpose?
Betty	Oh, we are saving up for a FUN-FUN-FUN-FUN-FUN-FUN trip to Lost-In-The-Woods Provincial Park.
Prophet	There must be a lot of stress for you in this.
Betty	O dear yes, I'm always afraid we'll run out of food.
Prophet	(Compassionately) Betty, may the fire of the Spirit touch you and your people, so that you want to truly meet this Jesus Christ. May the wind of the Spirit stir you to talk about the gospel – among yourselves, and with your non-church friends. (Prophet holds hand out in blessing as Betty exits.)

(Enter Mrs. Many Meetings, who flips through a little date book in puzzlement.)

Mrs M.M.	(Caught by surprise) Oh, hello. I'm just trying to figure out which meeting I'm going to.
Prophet	You're Mrs. Many Meetings, I think. You have served the church well, Mrs. Meetings.
Mrs M.M.	I take joy in serving. We're always raising money for something. Last year we replaced the carpet in the church lounge – you know after the youth group had one of their FUN-FUN nights. (turns and glares at Betty Busy Feet)
Prophet	Is there more?
Mrs M.M.	Definitely. The oven and the fridge in the church kitchen need cleaning too. There's always something!

Prophet	Does the Spirit call you to more than this?
Mrs M.M.	Absolutely. We hold two rummage sales a year too.
Prophet	Does the Holy Spirit stir your women?
Mrs M.M.	Several groups meet monthly. Mind you, the membership hasn't changed for some time. People want to meet with their friends.
Prophet	How could you reach out?
Mrs M.M.	Well, we iron the tablecloths for the communion table.
Prophet	How does the Holy Spirit touch you?
Mrs M.M.	The Spirit gave us a new idea recently.
Prophet	Oh?
Mrs M.M.	Yes, we decided to change all the locks on the cupboards. Too many things had gone missing.
Prophet	What else do you seek to do?
Mrs M.M.	I hope you're not going to suggest something more. We're all very busy.
Prophet	(Compassionately) Mrs. Meetings, may the fire of the Spirit move you to talk about your faith with one another. May the holy winds of the Spirit open up your circles to welcome in new people. (Prophet holds hand out in blessing as Mrs. Meetings moves away.)

	(Enter Cindi (and her friends) with Walkman headsets, bopping to the music – chewing gum vigorously.)
Prophet	Welcome to my place! Do you come seeking?
Cindi	I love music. I'm always on the lookout for new music!

Prophet	What is it you seek in your life, Cindi?
Cindi	I don't know. I'm not sure what adults have to share. Sometimes church can be pretty boring, you know. It is so predictable. I could go through the service in my sleep, you know. And that minister just goes, blah, blah, blah. I wonder if they feel it? Is it real for them?
Prophet	Do you feel Jesus, the Christ, is real for you, Cindi?
Cindi	Yes, but I wonder what do I get out of this? Is it worth the effort?
Prophet	What does Jesus Christ ask you to give, Cindi?
Cindi	Give? I'm not sure? But I know I'd like some clues about where I am going. I want to know I am safe in this world. I wish I knew what the future held.
Prophet	I know, Christians over the ages have wished this. In this relationship, or journey, what do you have to give this Christ?
Cindi	Give? None of my friends talk about giving... (pausing thoughtfully) ... or commitment.
Prophet	(Compassionately) I understand Cindi. And here is my prayer for you. May the fire of the Spirit wrap you in the love of God, for you are a child of God. You are truly safe on this journey with Jesus Christ. May the wind of the Spirit stir in you a gospel faith, and a boldness in talking about that faith. Go and let the Spirit truly touch you.
Cindi	See you later. (Prophet holds hand out in blessing as Cindi moves away.)

Bill Kool	(saunters in casually with his putter and golf ball) Well, hello! I understand you're the prophet.
Prophet	Yes, do you come seeking?

Bill	Oh, I'm not really seeking. I'm just wondering about some things. (As he practices his putting stroke)
Prophet	What is it you wonder about, Bill Kool?
Bill	Well, I'm too busy, you know, to get really involved in a church? But I wonder what makes these people tick. I mean what do they get out of this worship, and why do they meet week after week? I mean, I don't really need it. I just wondered.
Prophet	Bill, have you found a place where faith can grow in you and people to share it with?
Bill	Oh, I think faith is a private matter. (Practicing his putting stroke) I don't need to share it with anyone.
Prophet	And with whom do you worship and praise?
Bill	Oh, I think I can worship anywhere — on greens, fairways. I don't need to go to church.
Prophet	And how do you keep this fire alive in you, the fire of faith? It can be pretty lonely walking the way of faith alone!
Bill	I do get pretty distracted at times – missing putts – but, I'm not sure these church people are all they pretend to be. I know a guy at work who goes to church, but he's sure not perfect at work.
Prophet	Never mind the ones who aren't perfect, Bill. Is there fire in your own faith – in your life?
Bill	I'm not sure about fire? I wouldn't want to get too emotional about all this. That can get you into trouble too.
Prophet	Perhaps, Bill, you are ready to open your life, to receive. Most of all, the God of Jesus Christ, has some gifts to give you.
Bill	I wouldn't mind having the energy and hope I see in some Christians. I would like the excitement I sense some Christians have – just for life, for loving.

Prophet	(Compassionately) Bill, may you and your whole generation be touched by fire, so that you can know the passion and enthusiasm of the gospel. May the wind of the Spirit blow away your caution, that you can enter in to give and receive. (Bill drifts to the edge of the platform, as the prophet holds hand out in blessing.)
Closing	The prophet takes the candle off the communion table and places it on a small table by the prophet's chair. Then, with open arms she beckons the actors who are on the edge of the platform area. Gathering around, they form a semicircle, open to the congregation's vision, with the candle in the centre. The participants in the drama light their candles from the candle. Still open to the congregation, they step back, hold their candles up and sing one verse of "Breathe on me Breath of God" (or "Spirit of Gentleness"). (Note: a soloist or the choir can also sing this verse.) The prophet sends them out into the congregation declaring "Take this fire and share it." Then they move down each aisle of the congregation, taking the lit candles with them. With their free hand they touch people at the outer edge of each aisle on top of the head, giving them a commissioning, "Go and share the fire of the Spirit." In closing, the prophet stands at the center of the platform and declares, "Indeed, take this fire into all the world!"

A Pilgrim's Eucharist

THE GATHERING OF THE PEOPLE OF GOD

Submitted by Rev. Dr. Robin Pryor
Pallotti College
Millgrove, Victoria

Introduction

This service of worship draws on spirituality from the heart of Australian symbolism and thought. It invites us to bring our full senses to the celebration of life and faith. It has a poetic liturgy that demands our full attention, while also embracing spontaneous expressions of faith. At times we will feel overwhelmed by the language of the liturgy, at others we are invited to be spontaneous and bring our immediate concerns forward. This is a eucharistic celebration that could easily and wonderfully take place in a forest or bushland setting. *(Editor's comment: As with all the services in this book, users should feel free to adapt the liturgy to reflect their own context. In particular, North Americans may want to change some of the images to reflect their own geography, although much of what is printed here describes the beauty of Canada and the United States as well.)*

Preparation

Let us come to stillness in the beauty of this place,
in this vast and silent land.
Let us be aware of God,
alert to the signals of God's presence,
within us,
between us,
and all around us –
the sounds, sights, smells, the touch,
and the feelings, thoughts, and memories they engender.

Silence

Prayers of Adoration

We are invited to offer a brief prayer, or a poem from the back of this liturgy.

The Stones of Affliction: Openings to Confession

We are invited to gather small stones, perhaps to mark the sign of the cross on one's own forehead, then to place the stones in the form of a cross on the ground, naming aloud as we do, an affliction, regret, or confession. (Psalm 25:15–18)

The Leaves of Healing: Openings to God's Reconciling, Forgiving Work

> We are invited to crush some gum leaves, to inhale the eucalyptus aroma in our cupped hands, and to place the crushed leaves on the stone cross, naming the healing and reconciliation which we pray for ourselves. (Revelations 22:2)

Assurance of Forgiveness

> Christ Jesus came into the world to save sinners and redeem the whole creation.
> Hear, then, Christ's word of grace:
> Your sins are forgiven!
>
> Thanks be to God.

The Service of the Word

Readings

Shared Reflection on the Word

Silence

The Prayers of the People

> Individuals are invited to stand and name situations for which they are concerned.
> A time of silent prayer is observed after each situation is named.

The Sacrament of the Lord's Supper

The Great Prayer of Thanksgiving

> God, you spoke out a prayer that created all, out of the void, and the rocky heart of this sun-kissed land was a loving syllable on the lips of the Word.
>
> *In time beyond our dreaming.*
>
> God, you breathed a prayer into the diverse dry bones of all humanity, and the ancient peoples of this sacred land were a sigh of pleasure in the Creator's mouth.
>
> *In time beyond our dreaming.*
>
> God, you wove a prayer, an altar cloth of earth and living things, and the deserts, mountains, rivers, forests, their special creatures large and small, were sweet as wild bush honey on the tongue of their Lord.
>
> *In time beyond our dreaming.*

God, you brushed in prayer a bark painting of loving care for all that is, and passed its secrets heart-to-heart, in the living scripts of lives, and in age-old ochre lines.

In time beyond our dreaming.
God, you set the prayers to music in a manuscript of sand and rock, and a canticle of creation sounded down the songlines, breezed gently through the gums, echoed in the bird calls of lush rainforest and dry plains, and punctuated still night air in the beat of clap-sticks and dust-stamped feet.

In time beyond our dreaming.

God, you choreographed a litany of universal celebration, and, in antipodean fore-taste of new heaven and new earth, marked the place for newcomers, olive and fair, to be drawn into the dreaming of the love song of the Son, hanging on a Southern Cross.

In time beyond our dreaming.

And so we praise you, with the faithful of every time and place: we praise you at this sacred time, and in this sacred space, joining with choirs of angels, all who have gone before, and your whole creation, in the songlines of eternity:

Holy, holy, holy Lord,
God of power and might,
heaven and earth are full of your glory,
Hosanna in the highest!
Blessed is he who comes in the name of the Lord.
Hosanna in the highest!

Life-creating God
of pilgrim people throughout all ages,
of the walkabout people of this land,
of the journeying Christ
who is the Way, the Truth and the Life;
here again in new manna from heaven –
feed your people on the road.

Life-transforming Christ
of the healing touch, of the loaves and fishes,
of the Cana wedding and the Emmaus road;
here again in the bread and wine,
overwhelm us

with your meagre abundance,
your profound simplicity,
your unconditional love.

Life-giving Spirit
of the waters of creation,
of the quickening womb,
of the wilderness temptations,
of the tongues of fire
and the peace-filled breath;
here again with this bread and cup,
pour out your Spirit on us and on these gifts;
make the very substance of Christ's presence transform and sustain us,
as we hear and enact Christ's words:
"Do this in memory of me."
And so we proclaim the mystery of pilgrim faith:
Christ has died,
Christ is risen,
Christ will come again.

In this faith we are bold to pray the prayer Jesus taught us:
Our Father, who art in heaven...

The Peace

The Breaking of the Bread

The bread we break is a sharing in the body of Christ.
The cup we take is a sharing in the blood of Christ.
The gifts of the Exodus God, for the journeying people of God.

This is the Lamb of God
who takes away the sin of the world.
Happy are those who are called to his supper.

Lord, I am not worthy to receive you,
but only say the word and I shall be healed.

The Communion

Prayer after Communion

Awesome God,
who whispers in numinous silence,
in desert stillness and red-earthed horizons,

Challenging God,
who cries in the dispossessed and the dispersed,
in the stolen and the slaughtered,
Cryptic God,
who breathes life and hope in birdsong,
in canyon pools and stinging sun,
Disturbing God,
who shouts in sharp nails and rolled-away stones,
in ravenous dingos and crocodiles;
Companioning God,
who feeds us again in bread and wine,
in journeys outward, and the journeys in;
shock us into life!
nurture us into love!
and impel us with your grace
to share again and again, in myriad ways,
that vast good news: Christ is risen!

He is risen indeed!
Alleluia! Amen!

The Sending Out of the People of God

Blessing

Companioning God:
Bless us with strength from these age-old rocks;
Bless us with your stolen children's tears;
Bless us with the refreshment of hidden springs;
Bless us with the wild call of the magpie goose to live the Spirit's way.
Amen! Amen!

Some Thoughts on Pilgrimage

A pilgrimage has many interweaving phases:

- Sensing the difference between pilgrimage and tourism.

- Reading the signs "on the way," the pilgrimage as an entity, taking on a life of its own.

- Becoming aware of our companions on the way, and what it means to break bread with them (cum pane).

- Being alert to the story we are witnessing, its past, present, and future; social, spiritual, political, emotional outcomes.

- Moving beyond our role as observer, becoming part of the landscape, the story, the emerging memories.

- A more visionary appreciation of the landscape, reading its spirit now, recognising its "thin places" where heaven and earth, light and dark, life and death, touch and form a whole.

- Affirming the experience as a way of opening ourselves to revelation, the epiphany of this place and this time.

- Just touching the margins of another's experience, empathy beyond sympathy, awe beyond empathy, love beyond awe.

- Learning from deep ecology that all landscape has a presence and a memory, and that landscape records and speaks out what has taken place; it impacts on the sensibility of the people who live there, journey there, and there develops a symbiotic relationship between the person, the land, the Spirit, and the memories landscape has of others' footprints, heartaches and joys as they passed that way.

- Perhaps arriving at R.S. Thomas' question in his poem "Pilgrimages": "…Was the pilgrimage/I made to come to my own/self, to learn that in times/like these and for one like me/God will never be plain and/out there, but dark rather and/inexplicable, as though he were in here?" ["He is such a fast/God, always before us and/leaving as we arrive."!]

- Pilgrimage involves three processes: separation [removal from status quo, being intentionally set apart for a new experience, a theophany]; liminality [the crossing of thresholds into new ideas, cultures, landscapes, companions, and uncertainties]; and communitas [a deep bonding with human companions and with the immanent presence of the divine]. A spiritual pilgrimage implies movement to the sacred source of communitas, in space, or in imagination: this allows the pilgrim to return home to routines and challenges with a renewed sense of purpose and hope.

Poems and Prayers

Ripe Full Moon Dreaming

> Great Wandering Spirit, Soul of the Land
> and the Seasons of the Sky
> the Dancer in the Wilds on Fire
> and the Artist of the Ripe Full Moon
> come into this food
> and unite us as one
> as we share it with each other
> in remembering Jesus
> your son.
> Feed us with his love
> and his forgiving
> and help us to walk
> our communion.

Noel Davis, *Love Finds a Way* © 2000 Shekinah Creative Centre and Noel Davis. Used with permission

On Pilgrimage to the Heart of our Being

> Within the darkness of our being
> in the depths of our longing
> there burns a Fire
> the Source of our light
> the Passion of our lives
> the place where we are fearless
> and our worries dare not enter
> where our simplicity is recovered
> and our hearts flow wild and peaceful
> and all is consumed in the joy
> of our being
> one with each other
> in you.

Noel Davis, *Love Finds a Way* © 2000 Shekinah Creative Centre and Noel Davis. Used with permission

The One Story

The core of reconciliation
is the awareness
we are all wounded at heart
our love, our trust
and that we need the love and forgiveness
of each other
to heal our lives
to experience together the joy
of life renewing
that our stories at heart
are already woven
into one
and need but our acceptance
of your forgiveness.

Noel Davis, *Love Finds a Way* © 2000 Shekinah Creative Centre and Noel Davis. Used with permission

For Strength through the Day

Great Bunji God,
you sent your son Jesus
to be our Saviour, our Guide and our Friend.
At the dawn of this new day
we pray for strength to follow in his steps,
and to be true witnesses for him
among our people who love the great earth mother,
your gift to them from the dreamtime.
We pray for all people of all countries,
that they may become one great family
with Jesus as Saviour.
As we come to the evening of this day,
may we go to our rest in the quiet hours of the night
knowing that, in spite of our human weaknesses,
we have truly walked with Jesus.
This prayer we offer in the name of Jesus,
our good friend. Aralba.

(Bunji is an Aboriginal word for father.
Aralba means: I have spoken from my heart.)

Rev Lazarus Lamilami, 1910-1977, the first ordained Aboriginal minister of the Uniting Church. Taken from *Uniting in Worship People's Book*, Uniting Church Press 1988 Melbourne. Used by permission of Uniting Education – 2001.

DADIRRI...
DEEP LISTENING...
AWARENESS...
STILLNESS...

It is inner, deep listening
and quiet, still awareness
"Dadirri's recognises the deep spring that is inside us.
We call on it and it calls to us.
This is the gift that Australia is thirsting for.
It is something like what you call "contemplation."
When I experience "dadirri," I am made whole again.
I can sit on the river bank
or walk through the trees;
even if someone close to me has passed away,
I can find peace in this silent awareness…

The contemplative way of "dadirri"
spreads over our whole life.
It renews us and brings us peace.
It makes us feel whole again.

The other part of "dadirri" is
the quiet stillness
and the waiting.
Our Aboriginal culture has taught us to be still and to wait.
We do not try to hurry things up.
We let them follow their natural courses – like the seasons.
We watch the moon in each of its phases.
We wait for the rain to fill our rivers and water the thirsty earth.
When twilight comes, we prepare for night.
At dawn we rise with the sun.

I would like to conclude by saying again
that there are deep springs within each one of us.
Within this deep spring,
which is the very spirit of God, is a sound.
The sound of deep calling to deep.
The sound is the Word of God – Jesus…

Earth Day Service

Submitted by Elizabeth Beall, Director of Children's Ministries, Green Mountain Presbyterian Church, Lakewood, CO, USA.

Introduction

The children of the congregation (grades 1-6) led this worship service. Persons of any age, however, could be incorporated into the leadership structure of this service.

Five minutes before the start of worship, play nature music over the sound system as the congregation begins to gather. With regard to the set-up of the sanctuary, nothing out of the ordinary has been placed anywhere; throughout the service, however, various props will emerge.

One person walks down the center aisle turning over a rainstick as she/he walks. When the person gets to the front, she/he will turn around and face the congregation. This will be the cue for children to start processing in from the back, singing "Creature Praise" (by David Matthews, © 1988 by Word Music).

Children are wearing solid, brightly colored T-shirts, along with jeans, shorts, etc. Some choose to walk barefoot. Every child is holding something that represents the earth. Such objects include a variety of stuffed animals, a bowl of dirt, a pitcher of water, stones/rocks, squash, a bowl of fruit, etc. When they get to the front, the children face the congregation, still holding their things.

Call to Worship

Child 1

> We join with all of creation in worshipping God.

Other children (*One by one, children will individually lift up whatever they are holding in their hands and say,*)

> We join with the (rocks, bears, zucchinis, etc.) in worshipping God.

All Children (*When all the children have finished, they all say together,*)

> We join with all of creation in worshipping God!

Welcome
    (The following words of welcome were written on index cards, so that the children did not need to memorize.)

Child 1

Welcome to *(name of church)*. We are a community of Christian faith, trying to learn how to live with God, one another, and all of creation.

Child 2

You'll notice that we aren't using our regular bulletins today. That's because we're trying not to use so much paper. If you want a copy of today's service, you can ask *(name of child)* or *(name of child)*.

Child 3

Please take a moment to say hello and share God's love with each other right now.

(As people are saying hello, children put their various things (animals, bowls, etc.) down at the front and participate in the greeting time.)

Singing
    After a few moments of greeting, children gather at front again and begin leading the congregation in an upbeat version of Kum Ba Yah.

Use the refrain singing earth,
Kum ba yah
…wind, Kum ba yah
…fire, Kum ba yah
…rain, Kum ba yah

Hymn:
    "I Sing the Mighty Power of God"

Sharing Our Joys and Concerns
    During this part of the service, two children with microphones walk throughout sanctuary, so that people have an opportunity to share concerns and joys.

Four children will have been given index cards ahead of time that include concerns about the environment (both local and global), which will be read during this time.

Birthdays
    (This is a regular part of the service for our congregation. The globe is a new piece in it though.)

As people come forward for birthdays, one child will come forward holding a globe. As each of the birthday people share their name and their birth date with the congregation, the child with the globe will, in turn, say that today we are also celebrating the birth of all living beings: (such as "babies and bees, snakes and sunflowers…")

Singing

    Children's Choir: "This is the Day" (by Kathy Bowen, © 2000, Triune Music)

    Congregation: "All Things Bright and Beautiful"

Bible Reading: Psalm 104:1a,10–24 Contemporary English Version
(Read responsively by two children)

    Genesis 1: from *The Family Story Bible* by Ralph Milton, Northstone/WJK, 1996)

    (Use two readers, with a girl speaking as God's voice, and either a girl or boy narrating the rest.)

Singing

    Children's Choir: "Garden of the Earth"
                         (from a MacMillan Sign Language Textbook)

Sermon (Part One)   Feast of the Flowers

    Child   Today our sermon comes in two parts. The first part is a celebration of the goodness of creation. The second part is to help us think about what changes we need to make so that we can live in better partnership with the earth.

    A very short drama (approximately 3 minutes) from *Earth Child 2000*, depicting birth of flowers. Only the narrator speaks; the other children simply act out what the narrator says. We used the youngest children for this drama. (*Earth Child 2000*, by Kathryn Sheehan and Mary Waidner, Tulsa/San Francisco: Council Oak Books, © 1998. Available through www.simpleliving.org)

Singing

    Children's Choir: "Psalm 96" (by Mark Sedio, *All God's Children Sing*,
                         Wood Lake Books, 1992)

Sermon (Part Two)

Tons of Trash

We used the older elementary children for this drama, which is also found in *Earth Child 2000*. We adapted the drama slightly.

As the drama begins, two children are standing at the microphone with a trashcan between them. The trashcan is filled with objects that are commonly found in the trash at our church, such as Styrofoam cups, office paper, etc.

Behind these two children, on the altar area, are four boxes/bins, each of which is labelled with one of the following: Recycle, Reuse, Reduce, Reject.

One child asks the other,
"I wonder how many bags of trash our church family produces every week?" At this, four other children go to where we have hidden 12 bags of newspaper-stuffed trash bags. They bring these out and place them around the altar area.

The second child counts the number of bags aloud and asks,
"I wonder what we can do to cut down on all these bags?"

From this point on, the two children take turns pulling items out of the trash can, and talking about whether our church family can reduce, reuse, recycle or reject that item; then they put the item in the appropriate box/bin.

At the end of the drama, child one says,

"Let's follow through with some changes, so that next year we have fewer bags of trash up here."

Response Time

There will be baskets at the end of every pew. The baskets will be filled with cut-up pieces of office paper (used on one side) and pens. A group of children will be prepared to serve as ushers.

One child asks people to pass out the used pieces of paper and pens that are at the end of each pew. After the paper and pens have been passed out, she/he says:

"This is a time for us to think together about what God is calling us to do this week. Please turn to two or three people around you and take 2 minutes to talk with those in your group about how you might live as better friends of the earth this week. Be specific. Don't just say that you'll recycle more. Think about something specific that you'll recycle. Or maybe everyone in your group can agree to use public transportation on Wednesday of this week. The more specific we are, the more likely we are to follow through. Write down on your paper the action that you are going to take this week. When the offering pots come around, place your paper in as part of your weekly offering to God, along with whatever money you are sharing this week."

(After 2 minutes) "The ushers will now come around and collect our offerings."

Ushers will pass around terracotta pots (rather than traditional offering plates). During this time, nature music will be playing. Collected pots will be placed at the front.

Singing

Congregation: "Children From Your Vast Creation" (David Robb, Selah Publishing Co. This song is printed in the hymn booklet, *Sing Justice! Do Justice!* © 1998 by Selah Publishing Co. Available from www.simpleliving.org)

Children's Choir: "We Can Make A Difference" (by Neil Lorenz and Mary Lynn Lightfoot, Heritage Music Press.)

Words of Blessing

After the words of blessing, the leader will say,

"Let's join together in singing again the refrain from 'We Can Make A Difference.' "

Finally, the children take their plants, animals, etc. and walk out singing "Creature Praise."

A Litany for Graduates

Submitted by Mindy Ehrke
Bethany Lutheran Church, ELCA, Viborg, SD, USA.

Pastor   Dear Lord and Savior, you promised to be with your disciples to the close of the age. Be with us now. Guide and direct all those who are crossing important mile stones in their lives.

All   This is the day that the Lord has made; let us rejoice and be glad in it. (Psalm 118:24)

Pastor   Dear God our creator, smile upon all your sons and daughters wherever they may be, and especially we ask your blessings on these young people who are about to graduate.

Graduates   Every day I will bless you and praise your name forever and ever. (Psalm 145:2)

Pastor   Stir up your Spirit within these young adults.
May they observe your commandments;
may they hear your call to serve through their work;
may they know your grace and salvation;
 may their lives reflect your glory.

Graduates   For you have been my help, and in the shadow of your wings I will sing for joy. (Psalm 63:7)

Pastor   Dear God, you know how hard it is to send a child forth into this world. Grant joy, strength, comfort, peace, and hope to the parents and families of all those who are graduating.

Parents   What you have done will be praised from one generation to the next;
they will proclaim your mighty acts.

Pastor   Let us thank God for giving us these young people to know and to love: (the graduates are named individually).

All   All your works shall give thanks to you, O Lord, and your saints shall bless you! (Psalm 145:10)

Pastor   May all our celebrations be blessed by the Lord our God.

All   Let everything that breathes praise the Lord! Praise the Lord! (Psalm 150:6)

Releasing the Past – Embracing the Future

LEMONS AND HONEY RITUAL FOR CONGREGATIONS IN CONFLICT

Submitted by Rev. Muriel Bechtel
Mennonite Conference Minister, Waterloo, ON, Canada

Introduction

This service has been adapted for a number of different congregational or group settings where trust has been broken or there has been conflict and pain resulting in division and some people leaving. This ritual presumes some prior congregational processing which has prepared people to release the past and move on.

The ritual can be used as a separate event, or as a part of a regular worship service.

Materials Needed

Lemons cut into wedges or chunks in a bowl that can be passed around the circle; honey poured into individual paper cups (the size often used for individual servings of relishes) on trays that can be passed around; a large glass bowl half filled with water on a table in the front or center of the gathering place; a lit candle or green plant would be appropriate additions to the table.

Beginning Comments

(Often at the beginning, I read or tell the story of "The Nest," by Jan Bush, from her book *The Marks of the Maker*, Northstone, 1997. See page 85.)

All of us have memories of ways we have been hurt and probably also ways we have hurt others. We can all remember words and actions that have "set our teeth on edge," to use the words of the Old Testament proverb. We don't want to carry the bitterness and hurts of the past into the future. We don't want "our children's teeth to be set on edge because their parents ate sour grapes." (Ezekiel 18:2) We don't want our past to contaminate our future. We want to clear the air for a new start, a new beginning, a new future with our fellow members and our new pastors. We are all a part of Christ's body, the church, the community of the baptized, imperfect as it is, human as we all are.

That is why we have planned this time together as a chance to "pray our good-byes," as Joyce Rupp puts it. We want to thank God for keeping us through many changes – some painful, some joyful – and for bringing us to this day. We want to thank God who forgives what we cannot yet forgive; who graces our human

---

efforts, heals hurts, reconciles and restores us in ways that are beyond our understanding or power. We are still at many points on the journey, but we have come with a common desire to surrender ourselves and our past this day, and to offer our future to God.

Words of Invitation

Hear these words from the prophet Isaiah:

"Then you shall call, and the Lord will answer;
you shall cry for help, and he will say, Here I am." (Isaiah 58:9a)

Hymn: "Healer of our Ev'ry Ill"

Prayer of Confession
Over the past number of years, we have all worked hard and prayed hard. And yet, in spite of our best efforts and intentions, we have been hurt deeply and have hurt each other in many different ways. Often we have not agreed or understood each other. Let us each confess our part in all this to God.

Gracious God, hear our confession.

Our faith is uncertain,
our forgiveness slow,
our conviction weak,
our compassion wavering.
We hurt one another,
unintentionally, or with knowledge.
We exalt the proud and powerful,
and put down the weak.
We saturate the rich with good things,
and neglect the poor.
We send the hungry away empty-handed,
and help ourselves.

Grant that anger or other bitterness may not reign over us,
but that by your grace, kindness, and compassion,
every kind of friendliness, generosity, and gentleness may reign in us.

Show us your mercy, O God,
that we too might show mercy,
through your Son, Jesus Christ, our Savior. Amen.

(Adapted from *Hymnal: A Worship Book*, published by Brethren Press, Elgin Illinois, Faith and Life Press, Newton, Kansas, Mennonite Publishing House, Scottdale Pennsylvania.)

Words of Assurance

> If you remove the yoke from among you, the pointing of the finger,
> the speaking of evil,
> if you offer food to the hungry,
> and satisfy the needs of the afflicted,
> then your light shall rise in the darkness,
> and your gloom be like the noonday.
> The Lord will guide you continually,
> and satisfy your needs in parched places,
> and make your bones strong;
> and you shall be like a watered garden,
> like a spring of water, whose waters never fail. (Isaiah 58:9b–11)

Ritual Action

We have three symbols. We have pieces of lemon, reminding us of the bitterness of past goodbyes, the bitterness others have caused us, and the bitterness we have caused. As we pass the lemon, I invite you to take one, hold it or taste it, and name the bitterness quietly to yourself. Our hurt and our bitterness is an important part of your story, of our community's story. Offer it to God for cleansing, healing, and forgiveness.

The honey is a symbol of the grace that has been shown in many ways and places in our community. When you receive the honey, hold it or taste it, and take a moment to remember the grace and kindness you have received from others. Recall the grace you have given to others, even when it was hard. Name it quietly to yourself and honor it, for it is a sign of God's grace and mercy in your life and in our community. Grace too is part of your story – of our story. Thank God for moments of grace and kindness and understanding.

The bowl of water symbolizes the church, the body of Christ, those who have been baptized with water. What we are doing today will not take away our humanness. But it is an affirmation of our faith in God's presence, power, and grace in the church – cleansing, healing, and refreshing us – restoring us until we are once more like a "watered garden, a spring of water, whose waters never fail." (Isaiah 58:11)

Invite people to sing the hymn "Jesus, Remember Me" while the ushers distribute the lemons and honey to the people. Those who prefer to do so may remain in their seats and reflect and pray quietly. Those who want to participate take the lemon and the honey, and reflect until everyone is served.

When everyone is served, invite them to come forward prayerfully and squeeze the lemon and honey into the bowl of water, saying,

"Let us offer the past, both the bitter and the sweet, to the redeeming, cleansing, and restoring power of Christ, who is at work in his body, the church, today and every day, healing the past and creating a new future."

Prayer of Thanksgiving

Thanks be to God who loves and restores us;
who makes us like a watered garden,
a spring of water, whose waters never fail;
who grants us the love, power, and grace
to leave the past behind and move forward into the future. Amen.

Hymn: "Go, My Children, With My Blessing"

(From Hymnal: A Worship Book, published by Brethren Press, Elgin Illinois, Faith and Life Press, Newton, Kansas, Mennonite Publishing House, Scottdale Pennsylvania.)

Benediction

Gracious God, we go on from here
as witnesses to new life through your grace.
We face the future with renewed hope and deeper humility,
a stronger sense of the sacredness of all life and the dignity of all people.
Send us forth with your grace and peace
so that through us others may come to know of your love
and life everlasting. Amen.

The Nest

by Jan Bush, from *The Marks of the Maker*,
Northstone Publishing, 1997. Used with permission.

The first week of December, I found myself in the company of strangers at a humble retreat center in the Gatineau Hills of Quebec. The flight had been dismal, and the sight of the bleak winter landscape between Toronto and Ottawa left me feeling depressed and nervous. With the flame of autumn come and gone and only grey naked forest remaining, I felt utterly and profoundly alone, despite the noise of the engines and my flight mates.

My colleagues and I had gathered at the airport, looking for the folks who would drive us to our Quebec retreat, making introductions as we discovered one another by quietly eavesdropping on each others' conversations.

We were gathering together as a group of people hired to help local communities deal with the phenomenon of family violence. I was thrilled at the prospect, but found my nerves screamingly on edge. As a survivor of violence myself, I felt more vulnerable than my naturally extroverted personality could handle.

We got to the retreat center and started our work in earnest. We were encouraged to spend some time outdoors in the severe cold and light snow to look for a natural symbol of what we brought as team members to this particular project.

The first thought that came to my mind was a stick. I would find a stick and break it, to show that what I felt was my special contribution was my brokenness, my experience, and my memories and scars as a survivor.

But this was not to be. As I walked through a door I had walked through several times already that weekend, I almost ran into the branches of a tree. In the branches was woven an exquisite bird's nest. I was startled because I didn't remember seeing it before, but there it was – almost at eye level. And the Voice I hear from time to time said, *No, not a stick. Use this nest.*

I carefully removed the nest from the branch and held it in my hands, marveling at what I saw. In it were grass and little sticks and bird fluff, a long piece of horse hair, a bit of human hair, and a tiny bit of colored yarn – bits and pieces of other creatures, other life-forms, other lives – all carefully woven over and under and through and around by some little birdling's mother.

Bits and pieces, pulled from its own place in the great scheme of things – twigs from the branch, grass from the ground, fluff from the mother bird's own breast, a bit of horse's mane maybe snagged on a fence, a human hair from God-knows-whom, and a flashy bit of yarn from a mitten maybe knit by some child's aunt or granny or uncle for that matter – all woven into a home, a haven, a safe space for little birds.

And as I marveled, I thought of the bits and pieces of my own life – a life that often feels so broken, so fragile and yet at other times so unnaturally strong. I wondered at the thought that my life was not so much a broken stick.

Because of my experience of violence, I have worked hard over the years to find alternatives to it. I strive to be hospitable and deferential. I dread the thought of hurting others in the way that I was so very badly hurt.

Over the years, God has woven the hard bits of my life, the broken pieces, the broken pieces, the discarded bits together with some of the soft gentleness closest to God's heart. They've been woven together like this little nest, and that's given them and me a new purpose: to become a safe place for new life to come into existence. A place where a small and vulnerable creature can find gentleness and security. God has woven the pieces of my life together with every bit as much care and skill and creativity and flare as that mother bird wove that nest for her wee ones.

I presented my nest during our time together and shared what it had come to mean to me. I was overwhelmed with the thought: What a revelation. What a healing. What a gift. What a God.

A Mother's Day Liturgy

A REFLECTIVE PRAYER FOR MOTHER'S DAY

Submitted by Noelene Martin
Penrith, New South Wales

Introduction

An empty vase of water stands on a table or on the communion table at the front of the church. Before the service, 16 flowers are distributed to various people in the congregation. All the flowers are different colors and varieties. Each person is also given a piece of paper with the name of one of the women mentioned in the litany printed on it. Two readers stand at the front of the church. One person reads the sentence concerning the woman from the Bible. The other person then responds with the sentence relating to women today (written in italics). At the end of each section, the person from the congregation who has that biblical figure's name on their piece of paper comes forward and places their flower in the vase. When that person is seated, the next section is read. No one must move while the sentences are being read or it will be distracting.

Leader

The Bible is full of real people; people just like us. People with hopes and dreams who experienced disappointments and joys. People with faults and characteristics worthy of praise. People who tried and succeeded, and people who tried and failed.

Today on Mother's Day, we focus on the mothers in the Bible. Although they lived so long ago, they experienced the same joy and pain that mothers of today experience.

Litany

1. I am Eve. My son Cain killed his brother Abel because he was jealous.
   We remember mothers whose families are torn apart by jealousy, fighting and misunderstandings.

2. I am Sarah. I was an old woman when I gave birth to my son Isaac.
   We remember mothers who are older, but who still bear the responsibility of raising children and grandchildren.

3. I am Rebekah. I helped my favorite son, Jacob, to trick his brother, Esau, out of his birthright.
    We remember mothers who mean well, but who make mistakes.

4. I am Moses' mother. I hid my child so that he would not be taken by the government authorities.
    We remember mothers whose children are taken or stolen from them because of commercial interests or government policy.

5. I am Pharaoh's daughter. I found a baby in a basket and adopted him, raising him as my own child.
    We remember mothers who have adopted children and mothers who have had their children adopted.

6. I am Hannah, the mother of Samuel. I was one of many women who had difficulty becoming a mother.
    We remember mothers who, after many disappointments, are finally successful in being able to conceive and give birth to a child.

7. I am the mother of David. I watched as my son grew from being a shepherd boy to become a great king.
    We remember mothers who rejoice in the achievements of their children.

8. I am the widow of Zarephath. When my bowl of flour and oil is gone, my child and I will die because our land is gripped by famine.
    We remember mothers who watch their children suffer and die from malnutrition because of famine, drought, flood or war.

9. I am one of the mothers from Bethlehem. King Herod's soldiers murdered our children for no reason.
    We remember mothers whose children are tortured and murdered by soldiers and militia for political reasons.

10. I am a mother of Salem. I wanted to take my children to meet Jesus, but his disciples said not to bother him.
    We remember mothers who would like their children to know Jesus but who are discouraged by modern-day disciples who are annoyed by kids.

11. I am the Syrophoenician woman. Even though Jesus referred to me as a dog, I pestered him to cure my daughter who was very ill.
    We remember mothers whose children are sick or disabled and who will try anything to cure or help them.

12. I am the widow at Nain. Jesus raised my son from the dead so I would not be left destitute.

   We remember mothers who, as widows, or for other reasons, raise their children alone.

13. I am the mother of James and John. I asked Jesus if they could have a special place next to him in Heaven.

   We remember mothers who believe their children can do no wrong and deserve special treatment.

14. I am Mary. I watched my child suffer and die on a cross.

   We remember mothers who watch their children suffer and die.

15. I am Lois. Eunice and I taught Timothy, our son and grandson, about Jesus.

   We remember mothers who teach their children about Jesus.

16. I am one of many nameless women. I was not able to be a mother, even though I would have liked it very much.

   We remember women who, because of various circumstances, are unable to become mothers.

Conclusion

Leader   Before us is a vase of flowers, a symbol of the mothers we have remembered today. The flowers are different colors and varieties and at various stages of development, because mothers are not all the same. They are all different. Amen

A Christian Ritual for Affirming Pregnancy

Submitted by Rev. Kristine O'Brien,
Strathroy, Ontario, Canada

Introduction

Many expectant women and families are eager to be affirmed and prayed for in Sunday morning worship. I have found perhaps a greater tendency for this among those who have had difficulty becoming pregnant, and among families where there has in the past been miscarriage or trauma during pregnancy. When couples and congregations are open to this kind of ritual, it can be tremendously meaningful, a time of celebration and earnest prayer, a time of public recognition and a formal rite of passage for the family. This ritual is to take place in the context of public worship, perhaps preceded by a hymn as the woman/couple and worship leader gather at the front.

Accompanying Hymn Suggestions:

"In the Bulb There is a Flower"

"Mothering God, You Gave Me Birth," by Jean Janzen and David Ashley White (*The Book of Praise*, Presbyterian Church in Canada and *Voices United*, United Church of Canada.)

"God Who Gives to Life its Goodness," by Walter Henry Farquharson and Charles Venn Pilcher (*The Book of Praise*, Presbyterian Church in Canada and *Voices United*, United Church of Canada.)

The woman or couple stands together with the worship leader.

Lord, you molded and carved out the universe by saying, "Let there be..."
With one breath,
you gave life to a lump of clay;

With groans and panting,
you gave birth to your nation of Israel;
in the womb and water of Mary,
you entered into the world as Jesus the Christ.

And now your creating, transforming powers come among us here,
 making life where there was none.

All

We praise you, O God,
in your power and wonder!

Let us pray for _____.

All   Loving God,
When we hear the news
that soon there is to be a new baby among us,
we dance for joy;
we look forward to little hands and feet,
soft blankets and tiny clothes.
But we also know that being a parent
is hard and sometimes unrewarding work,
and that pregnancy can be an exhausting time.
We know that sleepless nights,
endless worry, and overwhelming guilt
accompany each new birth.
It is with this knowledge that new life brings with it both happiness and pain,
that we lift up _____ (&   ).
We ask for your help and strength
as she/they prepare(s) to become parents,
and as she/they endure(s) all of the strange
and confusing emotions of pregnancy.
Guide and teach us, O God,
so that as a community we might support her/them
in all that lies ahead,
and as we look forward to the day
when this child may be brought forward
to be baptized and welcomed in your name.
Bless this family of faith
as we prepare to make room for one more!
Through our Lord Jesus Christ we pray.
Amen.

Blessing for the Mother/Parents

The worship leader may (with the woman's permission) choose to rest a hand on the mother's belly.

May the God who created life in you,
the God who walks this road with you,
the God who offers comfort and hope to you,
bless you with peace, joy,
and a gentle presence,
throughout your pregnancy and birth.
Amen.

Thanksgiving for God's Gift of a Child

Submitted by
Rev. David Rathgen
Healesville, Victoria

Introduction

These services are an opportunity for parents and families to give thanks to God for the birth.

They are designed to celebrate the birth of a child into God's world; to give the child its own personal name; to bless the child with the gifts of God; to support and encourage the family as it thanks God for the gift of a child to them, and to welcome the child into the church community.

Some parents may take this opportunity to pray for themselves and for the continued well-being of their child.

These services do not replace baptism, but are usually preliminary to baptism. Baptism remains a sacrament of the church which is prepared for by a process called catechism. Baptism may be undertaken at any age – whether as an infant, youth, adult, or in old age. Provision is made here for those who wish to be baptized to become enrolled in the process of catechism in preparation for baptism.

Each service may be used by itself or else within the context of another church service such as morning prayer or Communion. If used within the context of communion, it should take place from the "Ministry of the Word" until the end of the prayers with the addition of the "Creed" and "Confession."

First Form is for use in private at a hospital or at the family home or a similar location, but may also be used at church.

Second Form is appropriate when the celebration takes place at church.

Thanksgiving for the Birth of a Child

THE GATHERING OF THE COMMUNITY

The minister may welcome family and friends with these or similar words:

> In the name of God, the giver of life who creates and loves us all.
> Dear friends in Christ, we have come to celebrate the gift of God to us in the gift of this child, born into the world, given to us to love, to nurture, and to enjoy.
>
> It is good to give thanks to God
> for God's love endures forever.
> Praise the Lord, my soul.
> And do not forget all God's benefits,
> the one who is kind and gracious to everybody,
> whose love extends to all people.
> Glory and honor and power are yours, O Lord,
> for you created all things,
> and by your will they have their being.
>
> God, the giver of life, we thank you and praise you for the gift of this child. Give wisdom and strength to those who nurture her/him that they may, by your example, lead their child to Christ. We ask this through Christ our Lord. Amen.

The Ministry of the Word:
Either Psalm 127 or Psalm 103 or Psalm 100 may be read.
Either 1 Samuel 2:1–10; or Mark 10:13–16; or Luke 1:46–55;
or Luke 2:21–32 is also read.

Homily The minister may speak to the people.

The Naming

The minister asks:

What name do you give this child?

From this day forward we shall know you by your name [names]

or

We have named you [names]

NOTE. Holy water may be sprinkled upon both the child and the family. Water is used as a symbol of God's refreshment, of our restoration to normal family life and activity; and as a reminder of our dependence upon water to sustain life.

The minister lays his hand on her/him:

Great God of heaven and earth, from whom every family on earth receives its true name; bless now this child whom we have named [Name]. (Ephesians 3:14–15)

The God who created you, who sent The Christ to redeem you, and The Holy Spirit to dwell in you – may this God watch over you, enabling you to seek, to find and to know your Savior, through Jesus Christ our Lord. Amen.

The Welcome:

The child may be dressed in special clothes:

God our righteousness, may this child, whom we have named [name], be clothed with your compassion and your kindness; with your humility and with your gentleness and patience. (Colossians 3:12–14)

The child may be presented with a candle:

God, who brought light out of darkness, and brought Christ into the world that all should see the truth; may this child, whom we have named [name], be drawn to the light of Christ, that he may be a lamp to her/his feet and a light to her/his path. (Psalm 19:105; John 1:9)

The child may be anointed with oil:

Sovereign Lord of the universe, who has created oil with which to anoint us, may this child, whom we have named [name], be crowned with your beauty; pour out upon her/him your own oil of gladness; may she/he be healthy and strong, protected from all harm, and ever live to sing your praises. (Isaiah 61:3)

The family and friends may give their own gifts to the child:

God of all grace, you want only the best for us and give yourself generously to us; may this child, whom we have named [name], always be rich in good deeds, generous and willing to share, so that she/he may lay up treasures in heaven where rust and moth cannot destroy. (1 Timothy 6:17–19)

A gospel is presented with these words:

Receive this book; in it is the good news of God's love. Read it, for it tells how you and your family can share in eternal life, through repentance and faith in Jesus Christ.

The family may bless the child:

God our Creator, you have made each of us in every part.
Bless [name] through and through,
that she/he may delight to serve you to the full.
Bless her/his eyes, that she/he may discern the beauty you give,
Bless her/his ears, that she/he may hear the music of your sounds,
Bless her/his sense of smell, that your fragrance may fill her/his being,
Bless her/his lips, that she/he may speak your truth and sing your joy,
Bless her/his hands, that she/he may delight to do your will,
Bless her/his feet, that she/he may be a messenger of your peace,
Bless her/his imagination, that she/he may be fired with the wonder of your world,
Bless her/his heart, that she/he may be filled with your love.
Bless her/him through and through, that she/he may delight to serve you to the full; through Jesus Christ, who took our nature to make us whole. Amen.

The Prayers

Any of the following prayers may be used here:

The family and friends may pray using their own words. Other prayers may be used.

The Parents' Thanksgiving
God our creator, thank you for the waiting and the joy, thank you for new life and for parenthood, thank you for your gift to us of [name], whom you have entrusted to our care. May we be patient and understanding, ready to guide and to forgive, that in our love [name] may know your love. May she/he learn to love your world and the whole family of your children, through Christ our life. Amen.

For the Family

God our almighty creator, eternal spirit, earth-maker, pain-bearer, life-giver, as you embraced your earthly home at Nazareth, so may this family's home be a place of your presence, your forgiveness and your freedom. May your will be done in them and through them this day and forever. Amen.

The mother may pray in these or similar words

Creator Spirit, I thank you for the experience of giving birth; for the preparation and expectancy, and for my part in your creation. I thank you for sustaining me through the pain of labor, and for the birth of [name].

Grant to me the courage and strength I need to be to this child a reflection of your motherly strength and grace. Amen.

The father may pray in these or similar words

Living God, I thank you for the gift of [name], this new member of our family, and for the promise of her/his personality.

Guard her/him from all harm, make her/him happy in receiving and giving love. Grant to me the affection and love I need, to be to this child a reflection of your fatherly strength and grace. Amen.

The wider family may pray in these or similar words

We thank you, Lord of heaven and earth, that you have set us in family groups, with relatives and friends of all ages. Help us to respect and care for one another and for this child, so that in our family she/he may see and enjoy many loving relationships; through Jesus, our Savior and friend. Amen.

For the father of the child

God our refuge and our strength, bless [name] the father of [this child] or [name] with your holy Spirit. May he remember Christ who endured opposition and did not lose heart; may he be blessed with courage to face the foe and to defend the right; may he be blessed with holiness as he brings up this child whom we have named [name] or (whom he has adopted) to respect you and to be disciplined by you; may he be blessed as he prays to you for this woman, this child and this family. Hear his prayers; guide his example; inspire his heart with devotion to Jesus our Redeemer. Amen.

For the mother of the child

Creator God, who has given us the joyful task to reproduce after our own kind, yet to live in the image of your own character; touch [name] who has recently given birth to a child or (who has adopted this child), with that same Spirit who broods over all creation. Restore her to full strength of body, mind and spirit; cover her with your wings. When she feels low, bear her up. When she feels weak, encourage her. When she feels unable to cope, may she find in you a shelter and a refuge. Amen.

For the child

Dear God, you welcomed little children into your arms. Now take this child whom we have named [name] or (who has been adopted by [name] and [name] under the shelter of your divine wings; guard her/him from all danger; send your holy angels to watch over her/him; do not let disease or sickness come nearby; and grant that this child may come to worship you with all those who serve you in your church, our Savior and our Sanctifier. Amen.

All prayers conclude with both the Lord's Prayer and The Blessing.

The Lord's Prayer

The Blessing:

> May the blessing of the God of Sarah and of Abraham be upon you;
> May the blessing of the Son, born of Mary, nurtured by Joseph, be with you;
> May the blessing of God the Holy Spirit, who broods over all creation, nourish you now and forevermore. Amen.

Thanksgiving for the Birth of a Child

THE GATHERING OF THE COMMUNITY

The minister may welcome the family and friends with these or similar words:

> In the name of God, the giver of life who creates and loves us all.
> Dear friends in Christ,
> we have come to celebrate God's gift to us of this child,
> born into the world, given to us to love, to nurture, and to enjoy.
>
> It is good to give thanks to God
> whose love endures for ever.
> Praise the Lord, my soul.
> And do not forget all God's benefits.
> The kindness and graciousness of God is for all people.
> God's love extends to all people.
> Glory and honor and power are yours, O Lord,
> for you created all things,
> and by your will they have their being.
>
> God, the giver of life, we thank and praise you for the gift of this child. Give wisdom and strength to those who nurture her/him that they may, by your example, lead their child to Christ. We ask this through Christ our Lord. Amen.

The Ministry of the Word:

> Either Psalm 127 or Psalm 103 or Psalm 100 may be read.
> Either 1 Samuel 1–10; or Mark 10:13–16; or Luke 1:46–55;
> or Luke 21–32 is read.

Homily   The minister may speak to the people.

The Naming   What name have you given this child?

All   From this day forward we shall know you by your name [names]

                    or

                    We have named you [names]

NOTE: Holy water may be sprinkled upon both the child and the family. Water is used as a symbol of God's refreshment, of our restoration to normal family life and activity; and as a reminder of our dependence upon water to sustain life.

The minister lays his hand on her/him:

Great God of heaven and earth, from whom every family on earth receives its true name, bless now this child whom we have named [name]. (Ephesians 3:14–15)

The God who created you, who sent The Christ to redeem you, and The Holy Spirit to dwell in you – may this God watch over you, enabling you to seek, to find and to know your Savior, through Jesus Christ our Lord. Amen.

The Welcome   *Marking the chest with holy oil*

May Christ live in your heart by faith that you [name], may grasp with all God's saints how wide and long and high and deep the love of Christ is.
(Ephesians 3:17–18)

Marking the forehead with holy oil

May you [name] come to know the guarantee of salvation and be assured of God's kindness to you always. (Ephesians 1:13-14)

Marking the hands or feet with holy oil

May all you do, [name], whether in words or deeds, be done in the name of our Lord Jesus Christ. (Colossians 3:17)

Marking the lips with holy oil

May your words, [name], be full of grace, seasoned with salt, so that you may always be ready to give a reason for the hope that lies within you. (Colossians 4:6, 1 Peter 3:15)

All this we ask in the name of Jesus our friend and brother. Amen.

Taking the child to the door of the church, the minister prays:
We who enter into your courts, dear God, with thanksgiving in our hearts, pray that this child, whom we have named [name], may always enter into your church with praise and worship you in spirit and in truth.

*Taking the child to the reading desk or lectern, the child is presented with
a gospel or Bible:*

We who hear your Word, dear Jesus, pray that this child, whom we have named
[name], may also receive your word, for it tells how you long to share with us your
gift of eternal life.

Taking the child to the font, the minister prays:

God our true guide, we who have turned to Christ and who follow him, pray for
this child, whom we have named [name], that she/he may be born again, received
by baptism into the family of your church, become an inheritor of your kingdom,
and maintain the truth of Jesus our Savior.

Taking the child to the holy table

O Lord our God, to whom belongs all blessing and honor, all glory and power; we
pray for this child, whom we have named [name], that she/he may answer your
invitation and come to this table by faith to receive the body and blood of our Lord
Jesus Christ, which he gave for her/him, and feed upon him by faith with thanksgiving.

Returning the child to its family within the body of the church:

Take this child, whom you have named [name], into your family as God's gift
to you; receive her/him with thanksgiving; with the nourishment of God's holy
Word feed her/him; by the discipline of God's love guide her/him; and with the
power of God's Spirit may you live in harmony with God forever. Amen.

The family may bless the child:

God our Creator, you have made each of us in every part.
Bless [name] through and through,
that she/he may delight to serve you to the full.
Bless her/his eyes, that she/he may discern the beauty you give,
Bless her/his ears, that she/he may hear the music of your sounds,
Bless her/his sense of smell, that your fragrance may fill her/his being,
Bless her/his lips, that she/he may speak your truth and sing your joy,
Bless her/his hands that she/he may delight to do your will,
Bless her/his feet, that she/he may be a messenger of your peace,
Bless her/his imagination, that she/he may be fired with the wonder of your world,
Bless her/his heart, that she/he may be filled with your love.
Bless her/him through and through, that she/he may delight to serve you to the
full through Jesus Christ, who took our nature to make us whole. Amen.

The Prayers

Any of the prayers of blessing from the First Order (page 97) may be used here.

The Lord's Prayer

The Blessing:

May the blessing of the God of Sarah and of Abraham be upon you;
May the blessing of the Son, born of Mary, nurtured by Joseph, be with you;
May the blessing of God the Holy Spirit, who broods over all creation,
nourish you now and forevermore. Amen.